BLACK MAN'S GRAVE

Also by Gary Stewart
  Breakout: Profiles in African Rhythm
  Rumba on the River

Also by John Amman
  Surviving the New Economy (co-editor)

BLACK MAN'S GRAVE

Letters From Sierra Leone

Gary Stewart and John Amman

COLD RUN BOOKS

Berkeley Springs

First Cold Run edition 2007

Photo credits: pages 112, 128, 144, 162, and 178
by Y.S. Mansaray; page 40 by Umaru Mansaray

Map: United Nations Cartographic Section

Library of Congress Control Number: 2006909302
ISBN-13: 978-0-9790808-2-1
ISBN-10: 0-9790808-2-7
Manufactured in the United States of America

COLD RUN BOOKS
P.O. Box 651
Berkeley Springs, WV 25411
www.coldrunbooks.com

Fifty percent of the profits from the sale of this book will be
donated to projects for the benefit of the people of Fadugu.

In Memory of Alie Mansaray

Around the world, proliferating weapons and deep-seated anger are fueling conflicts that cannot be adequately understood, or combated, as the struggle between two teams, let alone between good and evil. Ultimately, whether in Africa's neglected conflicts or in the higher-profile attacks of September 11, the only defence will be to defuse the underlying anger.

David Keen

Contents

Introduction

LETTERS FROM SIERRA LEONE

The mood was bright in the dark of an April night in 1961 when Sierra Leone joined the growing ranks of newly independent nations. Shortly after midnight Britain's Duke of Kent offered congratulations on behalf of Queen Elizabeth II as the Union Jack gave way to the new nation's tricolor—green for the gifts of agriculture and natural resources, white for unity and justice, and blue for the country's magnificent Atlantic harbor. Fireworks lit the sky launching a wave of celebrations around Freetown, the capital, which lasted well into daylight. No matter that the disparate peoples united that day would just as likely—if left to their own devices—have chosen to form different (or no) alliances and, perhaps, not troubled themselves with the formation of a European-style nation-state governed by parliament and prime minister. Although they never had much of a say in the matter, the people of Sierra Leone were left to make the best of it.

On other shores the latter-stage, often-turbulent gestations of Sierra Leone and its neighbors played out, much to the fascination of the authors of this book, in classrooms and newspapers and on radio and TV. From different Michigan towns in slightly different times—and unbeknown to each other—we shared an interest in Africa. "It was this far away, exotic place," as John has said. "Ever since I can remember, even prior to starting school, I wanted to go to Africa."

The opportunity arrived for Gary in 1968. When confronted with the choice of having "to destroy a village to save it" in Vietnam or showing the world a different face of America through work in the Peace

Corps, the path to follow seemed clear. Through the luck of the draw he wound up on the west coast of Africa, in the north of Sierra Leone, in the small village of Fadugu. There he taught fourth grade students, raised chickens, and learned far more than he could ever impart.

John went to Sierra Leone eleven years later, after declining assignments outside of Africa. Posted in Fadugu, he led an agricultural education program aimed at primary school students, worked with established farmers to improve crop yields, and arranged funding for construction of a new school in an outlying village.

More important, our sojourns in Fadugu helped to forge lasting friendships with the people we encountered there, sustained long after we departed through a continuous exchange of letters. That correspondence forms the foundation of our book.

Most of our friends were born in the days of waning colonial rule, came of age in the afterglow of independence, and spent what had promised to be their most productive years trying to escape a terrible war. We wish to thank them—especially A.K. Bangura, Y.S. Mansaray, and Umaru Mansaray—for sharing with us their experiences of joy and sadness and their many frustrations. This is the story of an extraordinary period in the lives of our friends and their neighbors in Fadugu and, ultimately, in the life of Sierra Leone.

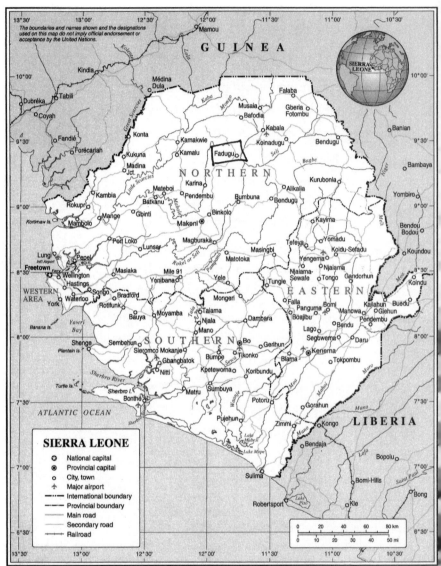

Prologue
Descent Into Evil

White man's grave, someone once called this steamy stretch of West Africa's coast where missionaries and colonial administrators routinely succumbed to the ravages of yellow fever, malaria, and dysentery. But for nearly eleven years beginning in 1991, black men, black women, and their children did the dying—most of it at the hands of their own brothers and sisters.

Unlike the early white men, Sierra Leoneans at the end of the twentieth century held no hope of a ship on the horizon that might take them back to Lisbon or London. No quinine or anti-viral could stave off the worst of their affliction. Theirs was a condition of continual misery eased only slightly by a vague hope that the world might take notice and send help.

The war that raged in Sierra Leone, the war that took the lives of thousands and left thousands more homeless, was born of the corruption and poverty that plagued the country since its independence. Like the crooked officials who controlled the government, the insurgents targeted Sierra Leone's five million civilians, killing them, raping them, stealing their possessions and even their children, turning some into soldiers who would commit more atrocities.

On March 23, 1991, a small band of armed rebels padded through the rain forest on Sierra Leone's southeastern border to launch a gruesome orgy. In the beginning the incursion seemed manageable. Writing from the village of Fadugu, some 200 miles north of the fighting, Umaru Mansaray, a farmer and budding businessman, echoed the Sierra Leone government's initial assessment.

I cannot say much for now except that there is a rebel incursion of the National Patriotic Front of Liberia [NPFL] headed by Charles Taylor in the south and eastern part of the country. Our brothers (Guinea and Nigeria) have joined forces to push back the bandits. Meanwhile, life is normal in the city [Freetown] and the north. Mind you only Kailahun and Pujehun Districts were attacked.

Umaru Mansaray
Fadugu, April 4, 1991

Soon after their first raids, the rebels identified themselves as Sierra Leoneans of the Revolutionary United Front (RUF) led by a cashiered army corporal named Foday Sankoh. But Charles Taylor, whose NPFL had been fighting for power in Liberia since Christmas Eve of 1989, bore much responsibility. Taylor had threatened to punish Sierra Leone for allowing a multi-national West African army to intervene in the Liberian conflict from a base at Sierra Leone's Lungi International Airport. He also coveted his neighbor's wealth of diamonds, which he could use to buy more guns and perhaps enrich himself. Although Taylor denied involvement with the RUF, it was inconceivable that the rebel group could have carried out its attacks from NPFL-held territory without his permission and assistance, if not outright instigation.

That Taylor one day would be indicted for war crimes seemed like minimal justice, for the conflagration he helped to ignite—what looked at first like a minor brush fire—grew to involve every corner of Sierra Leone and took one of the largest contingents of United Nations forces ever deployed to extinguish.

Chapter One

FREETOWN

For a few brief and beautiful moments, Sierra Leone's eleven years of agony dissolve as a visitor's plane descends through patches of puffy white. Outside the window thick mangrove swamps blanket the Atlantic shore then gradually yield to rugged inland grass and palm trees. A few moments nearer the exuberant landscape, Lungi Airport's slender concrete welcome suddenly unfurls below. These days soldiers of the new, British-trained Sierra Leone army control the airport, watched closely by United Nations troops in the country to support a fragile peace.

During normal times riding from Lungi to Freetown is a marvelous way to shift into the relaxed pace of African life—the African penchant for ignoring the clock has been the undoing of many a Western visitor who wanted things to happen with the promptness of London or New York—for Freetown lies on the opposite bank of the Sierra Leone River, whose broad mouth forms one of the world's finest natural harbors. A ferry shuttles new arrivals across the four miles of choppy water in an unhurried passage of striking beauty. In the distance, the city sprawls along a peninsula on a narrow strip of lowland between the water and a steep rise of lush, green mountains. The mountains and claps of tropical thunder inspired fifteenth-century Portuguese explorers to proclaim the place *Serra Lyoa*, lion mountain. In this harbor, thousands of Africans were sold into slavery, and beginning in 1787, thousands of freed Africans came home.

In 1783 an itinerant botanist named Henry Smeathman devised a "Plan of a Settlement to be made near Sierra Leone, on the Grain Coast of Africa: intended more particularly for the service and happy establishment of Blacks and People of colour to be shipped as freemen under the direction of the Committee for Relieving the Black Poor, and under the protection of the British Government." The black poor were London's free but destitute blacks whose presence was becoming a "social problem." With help from British abolitionist Granville Sharp, 341 black poor accompanied by another group of outcasts, 70 white London prostitutes, landed in Sierra Leone in May of 1787. They were followed, in 1792, by several shiploads of black Americans who had won their freedom by joining the British forces during the American Revolution. These disparate immigrants took up residence in the newly named colony of Freetown.

At the turn of the century, Maroons, former runaway slaves from the mountains of Jamaica who had been duped into exile after revolting against the British, joined the settlers in Freetown. A fourth group came after Great Britain abolished its slave trade in 1807 when the Royal Navy intercepted several thousand Africans bound for slavery on the high seas and deposited them in Freetown. The British government assumed complete control of the growing colony in 1808.

By the early 1850s a German missionary named Sigismund Koelle had documented 160 languages and 40 dialects among Freetown citizens who had come to the colony from up and down the West African coast and as far east as Malawi and Mozambique. Names of areas within the colony like Congo Town and Kroo Town reflected this astonishing diversity. The mix of peoples produced Freetown's Creole community—now called Krio—whose European-influenced culture and language—also called Krio—came to dominate the region.

Away from the coast, ethnic fighting that disrupted trade and the need to check the French, who were already well-entrenched in West Africa, moved the British to expand their territorial claims. Soon the indigenous Mende, Temne, Limba, and a dozen other nearby peoples saw their authority usurped by British rulers. Expansion became official in 1896 when Great Britain proclaimed large areas of the interior as a protectorate. Over the next sixty years, colony and protectorate, an area roughly the size of South Carolina, gradually coalesced under British administration into the country of Sierra Leone. On history's grand timeline it was an instant nation-state, an alien conception imposed on the people of the region. The British released their creation on April 27, 1961, and Sierra Leone became an independent nation with dominion status in the British Commonwealth.

Although English is Sierra Leone's official language, Krio is the language of everyday conversation. All ethnic groups use Krio to speak to one another, making it a great national unifier. Largely based on English, Krio is earthy, more direct than the mother tongue with a built-in sense of humor. Krio speakers have produced such gems of wisdom as, "If yu no no usai yu de go, yu fo no usai yu komot" (if you don't know where you are going, you should know where you came from). And, "Da tik wey man klem go up, na in i go klem kam don" (the tree a man climbs up is the one he is going to climb down).

Krio evolved from some of the same linguistic roots as Jamaican patois and the pidgin of Nigeria and western Cameroon. Much of its English-derived vocabulary borrows from the lexicon of British slave traders and colonial officials, with additions from plantation overseers in the New World. A multitude of African languages, Spanish, Portuguese, and French enhanced its vocabulary when the British began to intercept slave ships and bring the liberated Africans to Freetown. With British expansion, Krio made its way upcountry via Krio traders and the Krio clerks, police, and administrators who formed the backbone of colonial bureaucracy. Krio not only allowed the peoples of the protectorate to communicate with Freetown, it enabled them to speak to one another. Over time, they too contributed to its vocabulary.

Krio's birthplace is a hodgepodge of aged clapboard houses, tin shacks, compact shops, and sprawling markets. Seen from the surrounding hills the city's undulating waves of corroded metal roofs blend into each other, interrupted by an occasional high-rise. Vultures skim the rusty sea through pungent ripples of diesel fumes and the smoke of wood cook fires. Down below, the crush of buildings presses in on sidewalk-sized streets fluid with the tussle of cars and people. Everyone from beggars to bankers seems to stay outside.

An ancient cotton tree, said to have offered shelter to Freetown's first settlers, dominates the center of town, towering over the American Embassy and the formerly dilapidated law court building, newly refurbished by the British. Just up a nearby hill lies State House, a bland, colonial-era edifice that once housed Her Majesty's governor, now office of the president.

Shops that used to belong to Lebanese merchants line the main street, named for former president Siaka Stevens. Lebanese began to settle in West Africa in the early 1900s as they fled from Turkish rule in the days of the Ottoman Empire. Names like Bahsoon and Yazbeck and Basma became almost as common as homegrown Kamara, Koroma, and Sesay. Before the war Lebanese controlled commerce in Sierra Leone through ownership of the country's better retail shops, travel agencies, auto dealerships, and industrial concerns. Most of them departed as the fighting grew worse, and so went the country's economic infrastructure.

A block off Siaka Stevens Street, at the corner of Gloucester and Lightfoot Boston, sits the City Hotel, a favorite hangout of Graham Greene during the thirties and forties and featured in his novel *The Heart of the Matter*. In the old days, and right up to the end of the seventies, civil servants packed into the City's first-floor bar to ease the transition from morning to afternoon with a few pints of Star Beer or Guiness Stout. Then most of the civil servants moved to a new building away from the town center, leaving the City cheerless and empty. Today it languishes, a burned-out hulk, victim of a squatter's candle accidentally overturned on a May night in 2000.

Looking up from the City, Fourah Bay College, now a constituent of the University of Sierra Leone, clings to the top of Mount Aureol. The college was founded in 1827 by Anglican missionaries and once attracted students from across West Africa, giving rise to the mythic "Athens of Africa" portrayal of early Freetown. One hundred fifty years later it would become a breeding ground of opposition to the government.

In the hills to the west, around an area called Wilberforce, early British colonials built their houses in an attempt to evade disease-bearing mosquitoes. After independence such prestigious Spur Road and Regent Road addresses became home to Sierra Leone's nouveau riche politicians and their businessmen friends. Just beyond this enclave of largely ill-gotten wealth, Lumley Beach with its deluxe hotels, seat of Sierra Leone's formerly ascendant tourist industry, cushions the Atlantic surf.

Sierra Leone, like most African countries, experienced a steady movement of people from rural areas to its major cities in the years following independence. Food production declined in the face of an urbanization process that stripped the countryside of much of its labor pool and forced increased imports of rice, the country's staple. Fostered by the spread of Western-style book learning, the new urban class was a generation of office workers with no offices to work in. As a result the cities filled with educated unemployed or under-employed who were reluctant to go back to a life of manual labor on the farm. Others with little education also came to town in search of jobs that would provide a better life. But the jobs weren't there, and most settled into a kind of urban subsistence as occasional laborers and petty traders. Housing grew scarce, sanitation declined, and crime and prostitution flourished.

Freetown's population more than tripled from approximately 130,000 in 1963 to an estimated 500,000 in the 1980s. As the war dragged on throughout the nineties, refugees from the decimated countryside swelled the count to something in the neighborhood of one million. Some, like primary school teacher Y.S. Mansaray, struggled into the overburdened capital from the small northern village of Fadugu.

> I am still not teaching, and I have not found any other job yet. Believe me, there are lots of trained and qualified teachers and a host of others who have just graduated from college without

jobs. Many are finding it very difficult to make it up, especially here in the city. What has even worsened the situation is the current influx of refugees/returnees from the Republic of Guinea and internally displaced persons. Some of these people have been re-united with their families, and others have been taken to displaced [persons] camps. To be honest, life is becoming very difficult, and the fear of insecurity needs to be adequately addressed by the Sierra Leone government. I cannot predict when all these worst things would be over to make conditions of life once more comfortable. Really, some people still continue to suffer while other people continue to enrich themselves. The situation is really pathetic when one thinks about the general situation in the country.

Y.S. Mansaray
Freetown, Oct. 3, 2000

Chapter Two

FADUGU

In the days before rebels turned rural roads to deathtraps, the journey from Freetown to Fadugu still afforded a test of one's mettle. No matter where you wanted to go it made little sense to plan; in Sierra Leone things seldom happened at the appointed time. The best strategy was to set aside one full day for travel, be in the area where vehicles loaded, be there on time, and count on a long wait.

Government buses, considerably cheaper and more comfortable than the rear end of a private lorry, usually offered the best choice. Once in the proper bus station queue, one settled down to wait and watch the action. Peddlers swirled about hawking cigarettes, soap, toothpaste, underwear, oranges, water, herbal medicine, straw hats, brassieres, everything a traveler needed. Thieves mingled with the crowd, waiting patiently for their next victim's guard to drop.

A visitor would likely be taken by the impressive show of finery: women resplendent in ankle-length, wrap-skirt *lapa* topped with blouse and head-tie of equal luster; countless men in crisp Western dress, if not the stifling coat and tie, then slacks and a shirt-like African tunic; other men, especially Muslims, in traditional robes and fez-inspired cap sweeping majestically through the crush. No matter how threadbare, clothes would be laundered and pressed to the edge of endurance.*

---

* Foreign workers, generally held in high esteem by Sierra Leoneans, were regularly admonished by their bosses about long hair, beards, and sloppy clothes, as such dress would undermine local standards.

Each approaching bus would trigger a sudden scramble. The driver would climb down to hand out numbered slips whose purpose always seemed obscure since the order of entry depended more on one's ability to push and shove toward the door. Next, the driver sold tickets while another agent tried to extort money for each bag people wanted to carry on. Miraculously, all would eventually make it through the ticketing process, although not every passenger received a ticket. Perhaps that was some of the magic through which the underpaid driver and his apprentices survived.

Passengers jammed themselves into the aging Mercedes Benz buses, sitting three abreast on seats designed for two. Center seats, which folded down in the aisle, held one and sometimes two. Other travelers stood near the front and rear doors. At each stop, where even more people clambered on board, sellers engulfed the buses with a cacophonous offering of oranges, bread, roast meat, cakes, and bananas—curb service.

About 4 hours and 120 miles after leaving Freetown, the Fadugu bus rumbled into Makeni, capital of the Northern Province, to unload passengers and allow those remaining a last opportunity to buy food. Then it swung out onto the fine new Makeni–Kabala road for the journey's final leg.

One of the real achievements of Sierra Leone's post-independence governments was the construction of a large network of paved roads to connect major towns, and bridges to replace ferry crossings at strategic points (its ability to maintain them was another question). Unfortunately, the government generally undertook such improvements with an eye to some political purpose. During the lengthy rule of the All People's Congress (APC) that eventually led to civil war, development schemes largely excluded the southern and extreme eastern sections of the country, founts of Sierra Leone's agricultural output but hotbeds of resistance to the APC.

The Makeni–Kabala road replaced a dusty, rocky track that quickly dissolved to mud during the April–October rainy season, turning the fifty-mile journey from Makeni to Fadugu into a six- or eight-hour ordeal. The new ribbon of pavement snaked through chiseled "S" curves as the bus climbed from Bombali District's savannah to the uplands of Koinadugu. A few minutes north of the district boundary, where the road curved gently to the east, the aching behemoth would lumber to a halt in Fadugu, some twenty-five miles short of the Koinadugu District headquarters town of Kabala.

FADUGU OWES ITS EXISTENCE and its name to the migration of three ethnic groups—Limba, Mandingo, and Fula—and a nineteenth century West African war. The town's oral historians begin their mythic tale with two figures of renown: Alimamy Samori, a Mandingo leader skilled in battle, and Sara Baio, a Limba chief with strong persuasive powers.

Alimamy Samori Touré, a son of farmers, arose in the 1860s to forge a Mandingo empire centered along the emerald valleys of the Milo River in today's eastern Guinea. Samori's army was said to number 30,000 at its peak, and he used it with great cunning to expand and defend his realm. With the coming of the Europeans in the infamous "scramble for Africa," Samori applied his knowledge of the terrain and his natural gifts as a tactician to stall the persistent French and their steadfast Senegalese riflemen.

Samori traded slaves for horses in the eastern grasslands (today's Mali and Burkina Faso) to shoulder his warriors. Gold and ivory from his brimming treasury bought modern rifles and gunpowder in Freetown. The story goes that as Krio traders moved upcountry from Freetown with supplies for Samori, local chiefs (at the time called King or Queen) confiscated much of them as tribute. In response, Samori sent some of his lieutenants and their horse soldiers, known as Sofas, to Sierra Leone in 1884 to protect the trade routes. The Sofas, highly mobile on horseback and seasoned in the art of war from years of empire building, quickly took control of northern Sierra Leone.

Sofa occupation threatened Britain's influence over the peoples of the interior. Using Samori's need for weapons from Freetown as leverage, the British negotiated a partial withdrawal of the Sofas in 1888. In the early 1890s, squeezed between the combative French in the east and mounting British pressure in the west, Samori decided to regroup in northern Ivory Coast. As the Sofas began their departure from Sierra Leone, some chiefs convinced a few of them to stay. They would provide a fighting force loyal to the chiefs in return for promises of land and prestige.

Y.S. Mansaray, the grandson of one such Mandingo warrior, says accounts that were passed on to him describe his grandfather, Mamadu Mansaray, as "a very brave and determined fighter who was invulnerable to gunshots or bullets." Passing through Kasunko Chiefdom, the area where Fadugu was eventually founded, Mamadu Mansaray "was heartily welcomed by the then chief Sara Baio" and urged to stay on.

The Limba chief Sara Baio ruled Kasunko Chiefdom from the hilltop village of Katimbo, once a prosperous market founded by Fula (Fulani) traders. Visitors to Katimbo reported lively commercial activity as early as the mid-nineteenth century. Salt, slaves, and gold all exchanged hands there, drawing merchants from all over West Africa. Limbas settled in the village—said to have been named for its founder, a Fula called Timbo (more likely it took its name from another Timbo, the capital of Fouta Djallon where Sierra Leone's Fula originated)—when the Fula withdrew around the time of the Sofa invasion. Hilltop locations, favored by many Limba chiefs, allowed them to spot an invading army well in advance of an attack.

It might not have been difficult for Sara Baio to convince Mamadu Mansaray to stay in Kasunko Chiefdom. He would enjoy far more power as a Mandingo *mansa* (chief) in Sierra Leone than as a lieutenant of Samori who, by this time, was losing his war against the French. Indeed, peace proved profitable for the Mandingos who were as adept at farming as they had been at warfare. Mamadu's settlement, in lower country some four miles west of Katimbo, grew and prospered.

As Mamadu's grandson relates it, "The people became very hard working and engaged themselves in active crop farming like rice, potatoes, and cassava." During one particularly successful growing season "everyone was satisfied that truly there was an abundance of food for everyone everywhere in the village, and therefore eventually the people named it Fadugu, meaning in Mandingo language, 'a town where one is well fed.'"

As the British exerted control over Sierra Leone's interior, or protectorate, around the turn of the century, they divided it into five districts, each to be governed by a district commissioner. Chiefdoms within each district were headed by a "paramount chief"—the new appellation for King or Queen—selected from the ruling family, usually thought to be descendants of the chiefdom's founder. Lesser chiefs, known as section chiefs, presided over chiefdom subdivisions. The British district commissioner, disliking the laborious hike to hilltop Katimbo, persuaded Sara Baio's successor, Lamina, to move his headquarters to Fadugu.

Chiefs like Sara Baio governed the economic and religious activities of their people, allocated land for farming, and settled petty disputes. Under the British scheme of Native Administration, introduced in the 1930s, paramount chiefs were made beholden not only to their own people but to the white man, who began to pay them salaries and request actions that were often in conflict with traditional beliefs and wishes. *Chiefdom* eventually replaced the pejorative *native*, but the scheme continued, even after independence, forcing paramount chiefs to do a balancing act between their people and the central government.

Fadugu and Kasunko Chiefdom attracted new settlers during the years of peace and relative prosperity after the end of the Sofa occupation. Other Mandingos followed Mamadu Mansaray to the area, and in the late 1930s a wave of Fula settlers migrated to Kasunko from French Guinea.

The result of these migrations was a multi-ethnic community in which each of the three groups found its place. For the Limba, the oldest group in Kasunko, having come from Guinea perhaps as early as the eighth century, the land itself, the trees, rocks, and especially the bush, all have mystical significance. "Devils" (bush spirits) reside in certain forest groves or swamps, making them off-limits. While many Limba converted to Christianity, their bush societies still hold a stronger spiritual connection. Predominantly farmers, they labored in the swamps using *matchet* (cutlass) and hoe to cultivate much of the chiefdom's rice.

The Fula came to Sierra Leone to trade, find fresh pastures for their cattle, and teach from the Koran. To this day, cattle and Islam remain central to Fula identity. Their striking appearance—fair skin, delicate features, and slender build—readily distinguishes them from most other West African peoples. In Kasunko, Fula merchants trekked to the small villages outside Fadugu to sell sundry items like batteries, flashlights, and salt; they raised cattle on land provided by the paramount chief; and they sewed much of the chiefdom's clothes on old-fashioned, foot-powered machines.

Mandingos seemed to occupy a middle ground between the others. Like the Limba they are proficient farmers, while their origins in the Mali Empire, practice of Islam, and flair for business, link them with the Fula. Mandingos joined Limbas in their society ceremonies and prayed at the mosque with Fulas. Over the years, the peoples of Kasunko solidified their relations through intermarriage. Children played together in one another's language, and nearly everyone learned to speak the lingua franca, Krio.

After World War II, the British moved to streamline their authority in the protectorate by eliminating a number of smaller chiefdoms through a process of amalgamation. Kasunko and four other Limba chiefdoms were combined in 1950. Since Fadugu was the only chiefdom headquarters on the motor road linking Makeni and Kabala, the British designated it as headquarters for the newly amalgamated chiefdom, which was given the name Kasunko. Chief Alimamy Fana I of Gbonkogbon, one of the chiefdoms involved in the amalgamation, was brought to Fadugu from his headquarters at Kasasi to preside over the new Kasunko.

The government established a primary school in Fadugu following amalgamation. Later on in the fifties it installed a gravity-fed water system that brought clean, spring water from one of the surrounding hills to a series of faucets fixed about the town. A great convenience by West African standards, it eliminated the need for women and children to walk the half-mile or more to fetch water of lesser quality from the Maka River.

Fadugu's air, on the other hand, turns to grit in the dry season from October to March. Harmattan winds gather dust in the Sahara and deposit it as far south as the Gulf of Guinea, causing skin to crack and bonfires to burn to ward off the morning chill. Then the rain begins to fall again, more than 100 inches of it, to give the scenery a fresh scrub and fill the swamps for planting.

In the best of times, the decade or two after independence, Fadugu was a town of perhaps a thousand people. Its cement and mud-block houses stretched out along the road for nearly a mile. More houses clustered off the road in areas named for smaller bush villages like Katimbo and Kasasi where the people originally came from.

Traditional grass thatch gave way to corrugated metal roofing imported from Japan and Europe. Kerosene fueled lamps that breached the evening's darkness and powered an occasional refrigerator (electricity was a luxury accorded to a dwindling number of Sierra Leone's largest cities). Cooking fires dotted back yards and beyond them the latrines and bathing enclosures that sufficed for sanitation.

Chickens gave new meaning to the term "free range" as they ambled widely to scratch for food. Occasionally one would find its way into a neighbor's pot, but most seemed to make it home at the end of each day of foraging. Many yards boarded a goat or two, tied to a tree near a patch of grass.

A market for petty traders dominated the center of town near the foot of a towering mango. Nearby, shops run by Lebanese, Mandingo, and Fula traders fostered a thriving commerce. Over the rooftops one could see the lovely green hills rising in the distance.

PROTOCOL DICTATED that a visitor greet the paramount chief on arrival. Before the civil war, Chief Alimamy Fana Thoronka II presided from a compound near the center of town. A former chiefdom treasury clerk with a secondary school education, Chief Fana was the son of amalgamated Kasunko's first chief, Alimamy Fana I, and brother of the third ranking officer in Sierra Leone's army, Brigadier Achmed Thoronka. For a time in the late eighties, he had the additional responsibility of representing Koinadugu District's paramount chiefs in Sierra Leone's parliament. But, just as it happened with his predecessor, Baio Serry II, once Alimamy Fana had attained the position of paramount chief with its lifetime job security, his zest for work diminished in proportion to his increased thirst for liquor and young women.

At the east end of town, across from the chiefdom court, one of Fadugu's leading citizens, Teacher's Supervisor A.K. Bangura, occupied a house in the compound of the government-run primary school. His first name was Alfred, although no one could remember anyone calling him that. He was always A.K. or, preferably, Mr. Bangura.

One of a handful of Temne in town, the Christian Bangura had married a local Mandingo woman and fathered a sizeable number of children. He had come to Fadugu in 1966 from the distant village of Petifu near Yonibana on the southwest edge of the Northern Province. He had been an untrained teacher in those days, but after working a couple of seasons in Peace Corps training programs he enrolled at teachers college in Makeni. With his certificate in hand, awarded in 1974, Bangura rose through the ranks, becoming a senior teacher, then headmaster, and finally supervisor.

Bangura had been an excellent teacher, a strict disciplinarian who routinely employed the cane but who also prepared his lessons and managed to impart them with intelligence. He seemed to love children, and when he wasn't thrashing the resident Peace Corps volunteer at Scrabble or the town barkeeper at draughts, he could often be found on his veranda talking and giggling with one of his many sons and daughters.

Next door to the paramount chief's and across a side road from the market sat the home of Pa Saidu, son of the town's founder, Mamadu Mansaray. During the good times Pa Saidu's son, Yaya S. Mansaray or Y.S as he likes to be called, was one of A.K. Bangura's colleagues at the government primary school. Like Bangura, Y.S. had earned a teaching certificate in Makeni—his in 1978—and he came home to serve as the school's senior teacher, preparing Class Seven students for the examination to enter secondary school.

Y.S. and his two brothers inherited the family compound—two houses and a courtyard—when Pa Saidu died in 1986. A stone, said to have been given to Mamadu Mansaray by the ancient chief Sara Baio, lay among others marking a nearby area reserved for Muslim prayers. Legend had it that anyone who sat on the stone would find it difficult to leave the town. Y.S. had left, but never for very long. He was a devoted son of Kasunko who enjoyed a reputation of integrity, and, as the locals would say, he knew how to talk to people. These qualities helped him bend the ear of an elder or counsel a restive youth. Many saw him as one of the chiefdom's future leaders.

Back on the main road, just in front of the market, stood a small, bulging kiosk belonging to Mammy Thor Konteh. A woman of queenly bearing in her proper gown and head-tie crown, Thor was the savvy, elder wife of the Mandingo section chief, Alhaji Abu Bakar Mansaray. She had born most of Alhaji's earliest children, then relinquished that job to his younger wives and set herself up in business.

Thor began by "darking" *gara*, Sierra Leone's splendid tie-dye and wax print cloth. In the mid-seventies she moved into the shop of a departing Lebanese merchant to set up a large general trading business. When inflation began to gallop in the early eighties, she abandoned the general store to open her kiosk stocked with only essential, sure-to-sell items. The kiosk, perched as it was on an embankment overlooking the center of Fadugu, seemed at times like the village control tower. The boom of Thor's voice could often be heard, greeting a friend who passed below or admonishing a wayward child. She served cold sodas from an ancient fridge and warm rice from blackened kettles. And down at the west end of town her petrol station fueled the highway's gluttonous lorries.

Thor's husband, Pa Alhaji, presided over the family—four wives and more than thirty children—from Fadugu's largest house, which sat diagonally across from the market. A tall, austere-looking man, he turned faithfully toward Mecca to recite his daily prayers and strolled to the mosque across the street for regular Friday worship. His money was said to have come from the diamond rush in eastern Sierra Leone during the 1950s. Back home in Fadugu he had built his house, invested in cattle, and begun to assume a role in the chiefdom's leadership. A Mandingo in Limba country, Alhaji could never be paramount chief. Nevertheless his leadership as section chief enhanced his standing among all the ethnic groups. As the paramount chief's dissipation accelerated, Alhaji became the man to see in order to get things done.

Two doors away from the mosque, in a house as humble as Alhaji's was grand, the brothers Alie and Umaru Mansaray (not related to Alhaji) operated a thriving wholesale company. Both had attended the town's government primary school and gone on to secondary studies in Makeni. Alie returned to Fadugu at the end of the seventies to work on one of the government's local agricultural projects. He contracted river blindness (onchocerciasis), borne by black flies, perhaps while toiling in the rice swamps. The new drug ivermectin arrived in time to save his sight, but the side effects left his already slender frame wanting for some flesh.

Casting about for alternatives to his irregular salary payment, Alie began to buy cigarettes direct from the manufacturer in Freetown. Back in Fadugu he sold them at wholesale to the chiefdom's petty traders. Like his neighbor Y.S. Mansaray (no relation), Alie knew how to talk to people. His easy manner and endless repertoire of languages attracted a growing clientele. Soon he abandoned his government work altogether.

Younger brother Umaru went to work in the government-run Koinadugu Integrated Agricultural Development Project as a demonstration technician, growing vegetables and seed rice. The project's highfalutin name and lofty objectives masked its underlying purpose: to convince the European Community to finance construction of the Makeni–Kabala road in the heart of support for the ruling All People's Congress. The road was needed, so the argument went, as a means to get the agricultural project's envisioned plethora of produce to markets in the cities. Once the EC agreed, the widespread embezzlement of project funds came to light, leading to its collapse, but not before Umaru won a scholarship through its auspices to attend college at Njala in the Southern Province. He completed a two-year certificate course in agriculture in 1989 then returned to Fadugu to work the family farm and join Alie in business.

Farther west along the road, one passed the town post office on the way toward an area known as One Mile. A new Roman Catholic primary school nestled behind One Mile's houses. High on a hill opposite the school, Catholic missionaries had built a church to compete for souls with the long established Wesleyan church at the other end of town. Fadugu even boasted a fledgling secondary school, run by the Muslim Ahmadiyya mission of Pakistan.

A visitor to most any of the town's non-Muslim residents (Muslims were forbidden to drink), would be offered a cup of palm wine. Limba palm wine tappers—the acclaimed experts—would shinny to the tops of oil palm trees to collect sap in large gourds called *buli*. The process is similar to the collection of maple sap for making syrup, but oil palm sap needs no processing—"from God to man," as the Limbas say. The sweet milky liquid produces a mellow intoxication, and it normally fueled several hours of conversation as friends and neighbors gathered on their verandas to "keep time" in the afternoon's heat.

Despite the increasing burden of Sierra Leone's inept and corrupt central government, Fadugu, for the most part, remained a peaceful and prosperous place to live.

> It may interest you to hear that a common trading centre has been opened in Fadugu. It is situated along Kasasi Road very near the paramount chief's compound.... Traders around the surrounding villages and even far beyond—traders from Kabala, Kamabai, Makeni, and even Freetown—come to Fadugu every Sunday to buy and sell. On Sundays that area is like any of the busy streets you can think of in Freetown.
>
> A.K. Bangura
> Fadugu, Nov. 8, 1990

Less than a year later, however, the picture began to change. Continued incompetence in Freetown and the rebel invasion in the south aroused a growing pessimism.

> Up to now our government cannot even provide basic services for its people. Our standard of living continues to fall. For the citizens of any country to have a decent life will depend on a sober government. It is frustrating at times when one considers the role of our government in our own development.... For now I am working closely with Alie to run the business, because he can no longer run it alone. Even though the economy is unstable, we are still trying hard to survive.... It takes a lot of pain and sacrifice to undertake a business here at the grass-roots level. Factors such as capital, inflation, devaluation, etc., continue to be barriers.

Umaru Mansaray
Fadugu, July 25, 1991

Chapter Three

BIG MAN POLITICS

The time was ripe for radical change. When soldiers of the Revolutionary United Front attacked Sierra Leone's southeastern frontier they might well have been welcomed as saviors. In the months before gunshots pierced the veil of the rain forest, the people grew more and more desperate.

As you rightly wrote in your last letter to me, things are even worse with me than they were when you last visited me. This is now the fourth month without salary. The price of all our basic commodities has risen by between 300% and 400% [under a devaluation that dropped the national currency, the leone, to Le63 for $1]. Petrol which [used] to be sold at Le110.00 per gallon is sold at Le1000.00 [nearly $16] and kerosene [has gone] from Le90.00 per gallon to Le600.00. The price of rice is fluctuating because of the harvesting season, it is between Le10.00 and Le12.00 per cup. Transport is very high also, now it costs Le300.00 to travel from Makeni to Fadugu and Le200.00 to travel from Kabala to Fadugu. Our bus service is not effective.

This is the worst government our country has ever had. Everybody does what he likes. Smuggling, hoarding, and profiteering are just too rampant, and corruption is the order of the day. As you may have heard from radio and newspapers, our minister of finance has been dismissed. He was alleged to have stolen bags and drums full of our money. The system is just too rotten and corrupt.

Yesterday, our government announced that the country's two universities and the Milton Margai teachers college have been closed indefinitely because of suspected cases of students unrest. Very soon all secondary and primary schools in the country will have to be closed because teachers are not prepared to work because they are not paid....

There is no question of being shy or ashamed this time to ask for help. My family and myself are almost in a destitute situation, and I am appealing for help from friends and relatives. I welcome help of any kind. Of course I need not tell you the size of my family, seven of them are in primary and secondary schools.

My wife and children are asking here for special greetings to you. I am looking forward to hearing from you. May God bless us all.

A.K. Bangura
Fadugu, Nov. 29, 1989

SIERRA LEONE'S DESPAIR had been decades in the making. Before independence, contention between the colony of Freetown and the interior protectorate—colony Krios regarded peoples of the protectorate as their inferiors—had resolved to the disadvantage of the colony when constitutional changes in 1951 assured the protectorate of a majority in the country's legislative council. A loose coalition of protectorate elites called the Sierra Leone People's Party (SLPP) came to dominate politics as colonial authorities gradually expanded voting rights. The SLPP leader, a retired medical doctor named Milton Margai, was appointed chief minister in the colonial government in 1954 and prime minister of a British-style parliament at independence in 1961. Margai initiated what would become a tradition, the detention of opponents, when he jailed members of the rival All People's Congress (APC) who, he claimed, were planning to disrupt the independence ceremony. When Margai died in 1964, his half brother Albert Margai acceded to the positions of party leader and prime minister.

In 1967 the upstart APC harnessed mounting discontent among peasants, workers, and the young to win a narrow victory over the SLPP in parliamentary elections. Growing numbers of Sierra Leoneans had come to see the SLPP as a party of and for the Mende people, inhabitants of the Southern Province. Northerners—Temne, Limba, and several smaller groups—voted with Freetown's Krios and the Kono people of eastern Sierra Leone's diamond fields to elect APC candidates.

This same division soon became apparent in the army as well, when the force commander, a Mende named David Lansana, staged a coup d'etat. Although Lansana immediately lost control of the coup to opportunistic underlings, the military's intervention prevented the APC from taking power for thirteen months until disgruntled junior soldiers ousted their superiors and restored civilian rule. APC leader Siaka Stevens was returned to his post as the country's new prime minister.

Stevens had come to prominence during the colonial period as a principal in the country's trade union movement. He helped to organize workers at the Marampa iron mine near Lunsar in the 1930s and was a co-founder in 1945 of the United Mine Workers' Union. Stevens emerged as a moderate alternative, much favored by colonial authorities, to radical (in British eyes) Krio labor leader, journalist, and politician I.T.A. Wallace-Johnson.

Wallace-Johnson had been a thorn in the side of colonial authorities ever since 1913 when, still in his teens, he and his fellow officers in the Customs Department went on strike to protest their low wages and poor working conditions. Over the next fifty years, in Sierra Leone, Ghana, Nigeria, and England, he wielded his scathing pen and passionate rhetoric in the fight for workers' rights and an end to colonialism. When the time came, in 1946, to choose between Wallace-Johnson's candidate and Siaka Stevens for secretary-general of the Sierra Leone Trade Union Congress, there was no question about whom the colonial commissioner of labor would back. Siaka Stevens was elected to the post.

A son of the protectorate—born in the Southern Province town of Moyamba to a Limba father and a Gallinas mother—Stevens also began to dabble in politics. He helped to found the Sierra Leone

Organization Society, a group of protectorate elites who aimed to redress what they saw as imbalances between protectorate and colony. Stevens went on to become, along with the Margai brothers and others, a founder of the SLPP before breaking away to form the APC in 1960.

When Stevens finally reached his country's highest office, he possessed the age (63 years) and experience that Sierra Leoneans generally venerate. He styled himself as a man of the people, "Pa Shaki" the fatherly leader. He liked to recall his humble beginnings and still stopped at King Jimmy Market to haggle for fish. His benign visage stared from behind the counter in every shop and from every office wall in the land. But the country Pa had his city face too and more than a hint of avarice. He wore natty suits and a derby hat and carried a fine walking stick. He relished the title *Doctor*—he had received an honorary doctorate from the University of Sierra Leone—as he resented student opponents. And as the country slid down a worsening slope he built a hilltop mansion, the cost of which dwarfed his paycheck.

Siaka Stevens bears responsibility for bringing Sierra Leone to the brink of civil war. From his swearing-in as prime minister on April 26, 1968, to his retirement nearly eighteen years later, Stevens presided over the debasement of the military, the state, and the economy in order to enrich himself and to stay in power.

By the time rebels began raiding villages, the army was in sorry shape. Stevens, having survived the 1967 coup and two assassination attempts by a faction of the army on the same day in 1971, regarded the soldiers warily. Following the 1971 attacks he quickly negotiated with neighboring Guinea for Guinean troops to come to Freetown to insure his safety. Stevens then formed the paramilitary Internal Security Unit (ISU, known on the street as "I shoot you") as a deterrent to future coup makers. These Cuban-trained troops, clad in their red berets and toting AK-47 rifles, protected Stevens from physical harm and became the enforcers of his will. The ISU operated outside the law, setting up random checkpoints to shake down ordinary citizens.

The regular army rapidly declined after 1971, becoming an enfeebled agent of Stevens-style patronage where "who you knew" replaced "fitness for service" as the primary qualification among new recruits. Weapons, it was said, were locked away, out of reach of any enlisted man who fancied himself leader of a coup. The brass were co-opted with a constitutional amendment in 1974 that allowed the force commander and commissioner of police to take seats in parliament and the cabinet. Now the army could feast at the same trough as the politicians.

Like the army, the state itself began to atrophy as Stevens and his ministers gradually consolidated power unto themselves. Protocol gave way to patronage within the civil service (a process begun under Albert Margai). Supporters of the APC got the best jobs, often appointed by Stevens himself. Standards of probity eroded. Government officials padded contracts, negotiated kickbacks, and otherwise diverted funds from the treasury. The "vouchergate" scandal of 1981, in which several million leones were paid to fictitious companies for imaginary services, and its sequel "squandergate," the misappropriation of millions more destined for the administration of the provinces, were two of the most notorious schemes. The man who uncovered the scandals, Alfred Akibo-Betts, was later ostracized by the APC and severely beaten by thugs.

In the Sierra Leone of Siaka Stevens there was little justice. Only the most flagrant abuses by government officials—that is those that came to light—were prosecuted. Usually, after a flurry of investigations and preliminary court proceedings, prosecutors and judges whittled the charges into insignificance. Older Sierra Leoneans privately longed for the good old days under the British. "Black man no good," they would grumble as the contagion spread throughout the bureaucracy.

Each ministry employed "ghost workers," non-existent personnel whose salaries disappeared into the pockets of upper-level political appointees. Lower-level civil servants, whose inadequate salaries often went unpaid, began charging the public for services in order to support their families.

For villages like Fadugu the widespread embezzlement of government funds essentially meant people paid taxes twice. The headmaster of the government primary school passed a hat at PTA meetings to raise money for the purchase of basic supplies like chalk and exercise books that were supposed to be furnished by the Ministry of Education. If someone needed medical attention at Fadugu's free, government-run dispensary, that person had to pay the dispenser who hadn't received his salary for the last couple of months. If medicine were required—an injection of penicillin, or maybe some pills—that too would have to be paid for. As a result, even the country's offer of rudimentary health care dangled out of the reach of most Sierra Leoneans. At the beginning of the nineties, just before the war began, life expectancy hovered around forty years. For every three children born, one would die before the age of five.

Sierra Leone's state-owned businesses were also mired in corruption. The patronage-ridden Sierra Leone Produce Marketing Board, which sold the country's coffee, cocoa, and other crops overseas, routinely failed to account for what were estimated to be considerable profits. The National Diamond Mining Company, responsible for the mining and sale of Sierra Leone's leading earner of foreign exchange, oozed with opportunities for graft. Gems from NDMC tracts in the Kono and Kenema Districts of eastern Sierra Leone were easily siphoned-off for the personal gain of company managers, most of who were political appointees.

Stevens himself was widely believed to be involved in the illicit trade. In one notorious example from 1972, the 969 carat "Star of Sierra Leone" was, according to one former government minister, "taken out of the country mysteriously." Money from its sale, estimated to be more than two million dollars, was never officially accounted for. Stevens would later write: "I can take comfort in the fact that I know the proceeds of the sale contributed to a little bit more happiness in the lives of many." Who those were, he didn't say.

Although Stevens and his ministers surely benefited from such fraud, they also used a portion of their ill-gotten proceeds to secure a loyal following. Timely donations of money, materials, and especially rice, diminished the rumblings of discontent. Thus, whatever benefits accrued to elites and the masses alike were seen to flow, not from the state bureaucracy, but from Siaka Stevens himself. Even the APC began to languish as the reign of "Pa Shaki" became increasingly personal.

Sierra Leone's official economy mirrored the state's deterioration. Deficits mounted throughout the seventies as leaders tapped sources of government revenue for personal and political profit. The OPEC and skyrocketing oil prices also took a toll as the bill for imports of petroleum and manufactured goods soared and often went unpaid. The resulting scarcity of petroleum boosted the cost of transportation and led to periodic blackouts in the few cities that had electricity. High oil prices and declining production in the world steel industry forced Marampa iron mine to close in 1975, depriving the government of revenue it needed to pay its growing bills. Inflation took root, and the currency, once pegged at two leones to the British pound, devalued sharply. To help its public employees keep pace, the government increased salaries but then found it difficult to raise the money to pay them.

The most damaging blow to the economy came with the decision to host the annual Organization of African Unity (OAU) heads of state conference in 1980. It was customary for the leader of the host government to assume chairmanship of the OAU for the next year. For Siaka Stevens this would provide a prestigious climax to an extraordinary career. Budgetary prudence quickly fell victim to the imagined necessities for such an undertaking. New hotels were built and others refurbished. The conference center where the main event would take place needed to be upgraded. A presidential lounge was constructed at Lungi Airport, and modern ferries were purchased to deliver visiting dignitaries to Freetown. New lighting brightened city streets, and an OAU village, some sixty individual chalets to house visiting heads of state, was constructed. According to one estimate, the government spent $200 million on the project. "OAU for you, IOU for me," went the critique in the streets.

While wanton patronage helped secure the political future of Siaka Stevens and the APC, the party buttressed its position with a large measure of intimidation. Alarmed at the party's rapacious turn, several important members, including cabinet ministers Ibrahim Taqi and Mohamed Forna, quit in 1970 to form a new opposition party. A roller coaster of arrests and detentions later, both Taqi and Forna were tried on trumped up treason charges and put to death. Stevens in his public utterances routinely condemned it, but early on violence became an APC staple.

After the attempts on his life in 1971, Stevens had pushed a constitutional amendment through parliament that transformed Sierra Leone into a republic—the queen of England had been titular head of state since independence—with himself as executive president. He and the APC consolidated power during general elections in 1973. SLPP candidates, prevented by APC thugs from filing nomination papers, boycotted the vote, leading to an APC sweep of parliamentary seats.

Student-led demonstrations against the government at the beginning of 1977 spread throughout much of the country and moved Stevens to call for new elections. In a near rerun of 1973, most APC candidates faced no opponent while the SLPP managed to win just fifteen seats. Stevens's long-rumored intention of converting Sierra Leone to a one-party state came to fruition in the middle of 1978 with constitutional changes approved in a rigged referendum where the vote tally exceeded the number of eligible voters.

CONSOLIDATION OF POWER failed to temper APC ruthlessness as the citizens of Fadugu would soon discover. During the next general election in 1982 more than one candidate was allowed to contest each seat in parliament as long as the person ran under the APC banner. In the constituency that included Fadugu, local favorite Albert Kamara, a university graduate and son of the late Paramount Chief Baio Serry II, found himself pitted against an old Stevens crony named S.B. Kawusu-Conteh. Kawusu, who had previously represented a different constituency, carried the additional liability of being one of the few APC candidates who failed to win re-election in 1977. In that campaign, marked by extreme violence, Kawusu supporters had burned the village of Kurubonla while attempting to steal ballot boxes. Stevens assuaged his friend's embarrassment at the time by appointing him Sierra Leone's high commissioner to Ghana.

Although he had never lived in the Fadugu-area constituency he wished to represent, Kawusu lavished its leaders with gifts and promises of further support once he gained office. He quickly won the backing of Paramount Chief Alimamy Fana II and other chiefdom leaders close to the APC. Albert Kamara, on the other hand, conducted a grassroots campaign that courted secondary school and college graduates and the much larger population of uneducated farmers and petty traders. Looming over the entire process was the hushed remembrance of the Kurubonla incident.

On election day, polling booths, most of them monitored by teachers from area schools, opened throughout the constituency. Every booth contained one ballot box for each of the candidates, and voters made their choice by dropping a marble in the appropriate box. Early voting in Fadugu proceeded without incident. Then, in the afternoon, Kawusu supporters armed with knives and matchets attempted to steal ballot boxes at a polling station near the center of town. Shoving broke into fist fights as angry voters fought off the attempt to steal the election.

That night Fadugu became a sort of refugee camp of persons from other villages attacked or threatened by Kawusu's thugs. Acting as an election monitor, A.K. Bangura, then headmaster of Fadugu's government primary school, locked the ballot boxes from all the town's polling stations in his house at the school compound. Fadugu residents went to bed believing that at least in their town there had been a fair vote.

In the middle of the night soldiers from Sierra Leone's paramilitary Special Security Division (SSD or "Siaka Stevens's Dogs," the Internal Security Unit renamed for public relations purposes) arrived at Bangura's house to demand that he turn the ballot boxes over to them. When he hesitated, they pointed a rifle at his head and threatened to kill him and his family if he refused. They got the boxes and, literally, all the marbles. When the results were announced a few days later, Kawusu had won. Eventually even some of Albert Kamara's supporters felt resigned to the reality that success in Sierra Leonean politics relied more on influence, money, and violence than on legitimacy gained from grass-roots mandates.

Siaka Stevens's APC had dredged its thugs from the country's broad reservoir of young men with little education and few prospects who hoped to better their social situation by attaching themselves to powerful people. One veteran of the 1977 campaign recalled the tremendous sense of power he felt traveling on a motorcycle provided by his candidate, intimidating voters with a revolver and an array of knives, and taking from them pretty much whatever he wanted. The system in Sierra Leone was based on power not the vote, and it seemed clear to growing numbers that only power could overturn it.

BARRING OUTRIGHT REBELLION, the next best chance for change in Sierra Leone hinged on the president's health. Siaka Stevens would turn eighty in 1985, and his age had begun to show. Ever since the late seventies he had hinted at retirement from time to time. On each occasion sycophantic outcries from the ranks of the APC had "persuaded" him to remain. He dropped more hints in his 1984 memoir, and the following year he became one of the handful of African leaders to relinquish office before dying or being thrown out. Sierra Leoneans were euphoric.

In a slick move that seemed to insure a carefree retirement unencumbered by annoying inquiries into past improprieties, Stevens selected his loyal military force commander, Joseph Saidu Momoh, to be leader of the APC and Sierra Leone's next president. A one-candidate election in October preceded Momoh's assumption of power on November 28, 1985. The country had been delivered, at last, from the rule of Siaka Stevens.

Momoh was a rotund major general from Binkolo, a Limba village just north of Makeni. Through luck or through skill—it was unclear which one—Momoh had managed to weather the army's assorted coup plots to emerge at the top of the heap. As a career soldier he lacked a political base within the party he was now to lead. The battles that brought the APC to power were fought by others, including the constitutionally mandated heir, Vice-President S.I. Koroma, who saw themselves suddenly passed over. Nevertheless, Momoh began his tenure with an excess of good will from the people.

President Momoh appeared to make the right moves at the start. He proclaimed a "new order" in the country where the needs of the common people would rank first on his list of priorities. He launched a "green revolution" program to boost the production of rice. New agreements with the International Monetary Fund aimed to steady the economy. A largely peaceful, multi-candidate election (albeit under the APC banner) in 1986 produced a number of new faces and the return of vigorous debate in parliament.

Still, old habits were hard to break. Benefits under the new order regime continued to accrue to the powerful. Momoh himself set the example. He lavished money on his home town, lining its streets with lights that led to a fancy new presidential lodge and conference center. A scant two years after the leadership change, grumbling in the countryside grew louder.

> I hope you may have been reading African magazines about Sierra Leone, especially about the delay in payment of [teachers'] salaries. Last we took four months without receiving salary.... Since teaching is not a lucrative job, so teachers suffer greatly. This term we went on a go slow in protest over the deplorable condition of teachers in terms of salary and other allowances. The minister of finance promised to settle down every bit of our problems on the 30th November, but up to this hour I am writing you October and November salaries are still not paid. Teachers are the most wonderful magicians in Sierra Leone.
>
> A.K. Bangura
> Fadugu, Dec. 5, 1987

Farmers fared no better. Writing from college about his recent agricultural field work, Fadugu's Umaru Mansaray issued a dispiriting appraisal.

> The work at Makeni was interesting and educative. With the economic problems facing the country I don't think whether the government is prepared enough to help farmers to grow more. In fact what is happening is that most people are moving to the city now, leaving the rural areas in the hands of old people who will not support the country to meet its food requirement.
>
> Sierra Leone has turned out to be a lazy nation because people at higher offices think that they will make their fortune with government funds. Agriculture has deteriorated. The country has been solely dependent on imported rice. Do you think that will solve the food situation? A cup of rice now, per butter cup, is Le20. The average worker is [earning] Le24 per day. What will happen to people and their families?
>
> Umaru Mansaray
> Njala, Oct. 14, 1988

Despite what seemed to be President Momoh's desire to improve the situation, his new order resembled the old. One needed only a glimpse of the light that twinkled from hillside mansions overlooking an otherwise blacked-out Freetown to see where all the money was going.

A.K. Bangura

Chapter Four
SMALL MAN SURVIVAL

The people of Fadugu watched with growing anger as their hopes for the new order faded. Like their mansion-sensitive counterparts in Freetown, Fadugu residents had their own barometer of malfeasance in the flashy new Mitsubishi Pajeros—luxurious replacements for the old standby Land Rovers—that regularly sped through town ferrying some high-level official of the Momoh government to the district headquarters at Kabala. The shameless squandering of the country's wealth resounded like a slap in the face.

At Fadugu's government-run primary school, where the staff depended on Momoh's ministry of finance for its salaries, bitterness ran especially deep. A.K. Bangura, the headmaster for several years, had been promoted to teachers supervisor in 1988. This relieved him of day by day responsibility for Fadugu's school, broadening his role instead to include the conducting of workshops for teachers and otherwise overseeing the operations of government schools in three chiefdoms. But as often happened in Sierra Leone, the advancement proved illusory. With salaries routinely in arrears and no means of transportation at his disposal, Bangura found it impossible even to get to most of the schools assigned to him.

He had managed to hang on to his bungalow at the school compound in spite of the presence of a new headmaster who normally would have claimed the space. Work times, when he should have been on the road, often found him on his veranda pecking out a history of Fadugu's school on a cantankerous portable typewriter whose innards

defied the tropical marinade. He hoped the typescripts, faint for want
of a new ribbon, would eventually yield a book.

A teetotaler when he first arrived in town, Bangura had eventually
been seduced by the region's exalted palm wine. As morning bustle
melted into the languor of afternoon, he would begin to scan the
trickle of foot traffic just beyond his doorstep. There an occasional buli
would appear, artfully balanced on the seller's head. A shout and a wave
would prompt a sample, and if the wine were fresh, a brisk few minutes
of haggling usually clinched a buy. Buli in hand, Bangura would gather
friends in the side yard's shade to take the measure of another day with
no pay.

No matter how sweet the elixir, the responsibility for trying to
provide for his wife and seven children weighed heavily on Bangura.
The government's failure had placed this respected town leader in a
position of growing embarrassment. When a friend from the United
States came to visit at the beginning of 1989, Bangura was at the education office in Kabala in yet another attempt to collect the money due
him. He hoped his stranger, as a guest is called in Sierra Leone, would
understand.

> As you may have heard already, our government is still unable
> to pay workers' salaries. Of course, both primary and secondary
> schools remain closed in Kabala, and the government hospital
> in Kabala also remains closed. This is indeed a big shame to our
> government and a disgrace to the nation. Our office has gone
> all out to get money to help some of its workers but couldn't
> get anything. This type of situation may lead to genocide. Now
> teachers, nurses, doctors, and other essential workers don't go
> to work.
>
> On Monday this week, teachers, nurses, doctors, and other
> representatives from the various departments in Kabala had a
> meeting with the C.P.O. [chief police officer], D.O. [district
> officer], and other government officials concerning this delay
> or non-payment of workers' salaries. The C.P.O. and the T.S.A.
> [treasury sub-accountant] left on Tuesday to carry that report to

the president, minister of finance, and the minister of education. They are expected [back] this week. I don't know what the outcome of that report will be, so we are still very much angry over the matter. This is my first time to experience such a long disgraceful plight. This kind of situation has led us to go against some of our customs. In our African custom, the citizen is supposed to take great care of his stranger till he or she returns to his or her place of origin. We are not supposed to ask for any help, but at the same time our custom says when one has a good stranger the home will benefit from him. I am happy I have that kind of stranger.

I need not become ashamed [toward] you, because the situation has run out of hands. I would like you to help me get some reasonable amount of money so that I will be able to send Junior back to school and to take care of my home till salaries are available. We are expecting at least three months pay. I am sure we will be paid before the time of your departure, then I will pay you back out of my salaries. It is rather unfortunate that you should find me in this kind of situation. I am prepared to leave Kabala as soon as I hear your word. I deeply regret any inconvenience this may cause. Looking forward to hearing from you.

A.K. Bangura
Kabala, Jan. 12, 1989

Apart from the hardship its government-employed citizens endured, Fadugu continued to prosper, largely because of the construction of the twenty-six-mile Fadugu–Kabala leg of the main motor road. The first fifty miles from Makeni to Fadugu had been completed in 1985. Government officials trolled overseas for new money—every development project of any significance in Sierra Leone relied on foreign grants and loans—and soon put together a funding package with help once again from the European Community. The Senegalese firm that was hired to do the work built its base camp just outside Fadugu. Dozens of Senegalese workers with steady incomes and the need for food and shelter came to town. Dozens more locals hired on as laborers. The influx of new money came at an opportune time for the Mansaray brothers, Umaru and Alie. Alie's fledgling business that began with the wholesaling of cigarettes had expanded to include many staples of daily life like tinned and powdered milk, tomato paste, cooking oil, sugar, salt, and matches. Business expansion also meant that Alie could now afford to take a wife. As the rains abated and the crops came in toward the end of 1989, Fadugu's Imam presided over a grand Muslim ceremony joining Alie and a local woman named Salimatu Barrie in marriage.

Meanwhile, Umaru's hope for developing a large-scale farm had ended in frustration. Abundant, fertile land some twenty miles northwest of Fadugu remained inaccessible by road. Money from the American PL-480 assistance program earmarked for a feeder road to the site had been embezzled by Sierra Leonean officials. Loans, administered by Sierra Leone under PL-480 and similar programs, that would have been used to purchase seeds and equipment went to others who could afford the required bribes. Discouraged at nearly every turn, Umaru began to devote more time to helping his brother in the wholesale business.

Sales were strong at the end of the eighties, still one had to match wits with the country's increasingly contorted character.

> I have advised Alie to reinvest all profits into his business instead of taking it to the bank. The bank is not reliable. After you have deposited your money in the bank, they will not allow you to remove it whenever you want it. This has made the businessmen to hoard their money at home. The bank will not allow their customers to withdraw more than Le1000.00 [$16] each week. It takes me two weeks to withdraw Le2000.00. I have therefore advised Alie to buy more goods instead of taking the money to the bank.
>
> Umaru Mansaray
> Fadugu, Aug. 9, 1989

◆ ◆ ◆

THE MANSARAY BROTHERS were a small part of a colossal movement away from official channels. The country's burgeoning parallel market fostered a thriving commerce for those who could afford to indulge. "Sierra Leone's shops and street markets are well stocked with goods purchased by foreign exchange moving outside the banking system," wrote a correspondent for *West Africa* in March, just before the leone was devalued again. "While locally-brewed Star beer is hard to come by, the country is awash with cans of imported beer. Paying rates upwards of Le70 to the US dollar, the black market has the upper hand in competition with the banking system that pays only Le45."

In his fourth year on the job, Sierra Leone's soldier-turned-president, Joseph Momoh, found himself ensnared in a political and economic thicket that threatened to consume him. "Solutions to our socio-economic problems have always appeared intractable," he said during an APC party convention in early 1989. "This is because there is an entrenched and determined core of wicked and greedy economic manipulators whose main aim is to squeeze life out of the very country they feed upon. No sooner we move in the direction of solving one economic ill, another surfaces. This is the hydra-headed monster we have to fight; therefore we must engage ourselves in this fight with all the might and determination we can muster."

If indeed the president was sincere, no action by his government appeared to offer relief. The 1989 budget, with its stringent spending cuts and currency devaluation tailored to impress the IMF, simply tightened the screws on the ordinary citizen.

> I should have written you long before this time but the question
> of getting air mail [aerogrammes] and stamps is a big problem
> in our post offices in the provinces. One has to pay three or
> four times more than the cost so whenever air mails and stamps
> are supplied in the post offices they are hidden to be sold at
> higher prices. Our country leads all other countries in terms of
> corruption, bribery, embezzlement and forgery....

I have almost completed writing [the] history of the school, but how can I send you copies of the scripts when I cannot get postage stamps to do so. I have also written other short and interesting stories which I would also like to send to you for printing and production but there are no postage stamps in our post office in Kabala. I am trying as hard as possible to go to Freetown and fight to get stamps so that I can post them this holiday, or if you can suggest a way I can send them easily, I will be glad.

As you may already have heard or read in newspapers, our budget speech [by the finance minister] this year is the worst in the history of Sierra Leone. Prices of all commodities were raised from 100% to 900% and salaries raised from 35 to 55%. Bus and lorry fares have also been raised. Essential commodities such as rice, petrol [gasoline], kerosene, and gas oil [diesel] have been raised to 100% and above. My salary per month cannot buy a bag of rice while we eat more than one and a half bags per month; what a miracle.

> A.K. Bangura
> Fadugu, June 6, 1989

Dissatisfaction with the government burst into full view the following year when teachers, students, lorry drivers, and market women all staged disruptive strikes. People began to speak openly about an end to APC rule. President Momoh responded with the appointment of a constitutional review commission whose charge, it appeared, was simply to shore up the APC's position. But only its die-hard supporters believed the party could be rehabilitated. Cries for scrapping the one-party constitution and for a return to multi-party democracy grew louder. Meanwhile, events in next-door Liberia posed a new threat to the regime in Freetown.

ON CHRISTMAS EVE OF 1989, a band of armed dissidents operating from a base camp in neighboring Côte d'Ivoire, attacked the Liberian border town of Butuo. Members of the group captured by Liberian soldiers identified their leader as one Charles Taylor and said they aimed to overthrow the government of President Samuel Doe.

Doe himself had come to power in a bloody coup d'etat on April 12, 1980, and went on to preside over a corrupt and often brutal administration. Taylor, holder of an economics degree from Bentley College in Massachusetts, once headed the Doe government's General Services Agency—the central procurement office with its bounty of opportunities for the lining of an administrator's pockets. Taylor had fallen out with Doe in 1983 and fled for safety to the United States. Liberian officials accused Taylor of embezzlement, and at their request, American authorities arrested him in Boston. While awaiting extradition, Taylor sawed his way out of the Plymouth (Mass.) House of Correction in 1985 and returned to West Africa to begin the groundwork for unseating his former boss.

Just six months after its first attack, Taylor's growing army of conscripts and the disaffected, known as the National Patriotic Front of Liberia, stood poised to take the capital city of Monrovia. Then, two things happened to stall the rebel army's roll. A dissident faction led by Prince Yormie Johnson split from the NPFL, momentarily sapping its strength; and members of the Economic Community of West African States (ECOWAS) agreed to mount an intervention force called ECOMOG (ECOWAS Peace Monitoring Group) in an effort to stop the fighting.

ECOMOG—fielded from the armies of Gambia, Ghana, Guinea, Nigeria, and Sierra Leone and led by a Ghanaian general, Arnold Quainoo—got off to an embarrassing start when President Doe, on a September 9, 1990, visit to Quainoo's headquarters in Monrovia, was captured and killed by soldiers of the Prince Johnson faction that had split from the NPFL. Still the war continued as ECOMOG fended off the two groups of rebels and the remains of Liberia's army, all fighting for control of the capital.

For Sierra Leone, participation in ECOMOG seemed at first to make sense. The country that could scarcely provide for its own people strained to accommodate thousands of Liberians who had fled from the fighting. It also seemed increasingly clear that incalculable quantities of diamonds, at least some of which would normally contribute to Sierra Leone's budget, were instead being smuggled into Liberia to help finance the NPFL. The sooner the war could be stopped, the sooner those twin afflictions would be relieved. The Momoh government assigned 350 soldiers from its 3,000-strong army to serve with ECOMOG. In addition, a squadron of ECOMOG fighter planes was allowed to use Freetown's Lungi Airport as its base.

With the collapse of each successive ceasefire, ECOMOG's transformation from peace monitor to active participant in the fighting moved another step. Soon its Freetown-based air force began to attack NPFL strongholds in an effort to get peace talks re-started. An incensed Charles Taylor, speaking in November 1990 to the British Broadcasting Corporation, threatened to retaliate. Sierra Leone's Momoh, he said, would soon find out how badly he had miscalculated.

Taylor had a second reason to be angry with President Momoh. According to Sierra Leone's former foreign minister, Abdul K. Koroma, Taylor had come to Freetown in early 1989 (others say this happened in 1988) to seek the president's permission for the NPFL to launch its attack on Liberia from inside Sierra Leone. Momoh refused, and Taylor was arrested in Freetown at the request of the Liberian government. After determining that Taylor would probably be killed if he were turned over to Liberian authorities, Momoh allowed him to leave Sierra Leone in secret. It was a show of mercy he would come to regret.

Alie Mansaray

Chapter Five

WAR DOWN SOUTH

Somewhere in Africa, Liberia's Charles Taylor met Foday Sankoh of Sierra Leone. Their trail, it is said, had passed through Qaddafi's Libya, a plausible though difficult-to-prove assertion. Among self-absorbed nations of the wealthy North, such intrigues passed largely uncharted. On the ground in West Africa it mattered even less; a rifle bearing Libyan fingerprints was no more deadly than any other. What counted was the truth of their collaboration, for it was from the part of Liberia controlled by Taylor that Sankoh made war on Sierra Leone.

Foday Sankoh claimed to have been born "around 1936" in a village not far from Magburaka, the country's virtual center. Although he sometimes appeared in the fatigues of a revolutionary, Sankoh usually donned the robe and skullcap favored by Sierra Leone's elders. His outwardly calm demeanor and graying hair and beard made him look more like a kindly grandfather than a callous fomenter of mayhem. The way Sankoh told it, financial necessity had pushed him into the labor force near the end of his primary school days. Some years later, in 1956, he enlisted in Sierra Leone's army. There he eventually rose to the rank of corporal while learning the art of cinematography.

As a soldier Sankoh also observed the beginnings of the army's post-independence decline. "Those of us in the army were watching the politicians as they moved about in the barracks sowing the seeds of tribalism and politicising the army. So some officers became APC men, and others SLPP men."

The political virus that infected the army eventually felled Sankoh himself. His ties to Force Commander John Bangura, the alleged leader of the 1971 coup attempt against Siaka Stevens, earned him a court-martial. Although he denied involvement in the plot, Sankoh was found guilty, sentenced to seven years imprisonment, and given a dishonorable discharge. His lengthy incarceration—in the dehumanizing squalor of Freetown's Pademba Road prison—and Bangura's execution left him a bitter foe of Stevens and the APC. That future APC leader and president Joseph Momoh succeeded Bangura as force commander seems to have assured Sankoh's enmity. By the end of 1990, as ECOMOG planes flew out from Freetown to bomb the forward ranks of Taylor's NPFL, both Sankoh and Taylor eyed the government of Sierra Leone with a similar degree of hatred.

THE FRONTIER between Liberia and Sierra Leone meanders through some of the last vestiges of West Africa's rain forest. Although primeval forest once covered most of the country, cutting for firewood and commercial logging unfettered by any thought beyond immediate profit slashed the forest to near extinction. The descendants of elephants that once roamed to the outskirts of Freetown now sequester themselves in the remote southeast where the Gola Forest clings to life. There, beneath the towering canopy resplendent with monkeys, baboons, leopards, assorted reptiles, and a profusion of birds and bugs, the human occupants, mostly of the Mende ethnic group, have learned to live in harmony with the forest, cultivating rice in its swampy areas and harvesting the bounty of its trees. These forest dwellers would be the first to suffer Foday Sankoh's wrath.

On March 23, 1991, as thickening clouds signaled the approach of the rainy season, Sankoh's troops, a handful of Sierra Leoneans backed by soldiers from Taylor's NPFL, struck Kailahun District at the forest edge. They tested for resistance at two small villages, Bomaru and Sienga, killing thirteen people, eleven of them civilians. Over the next few days the rebels swept toward the northeast, capturing the customs post at Buedu and the bustling market town of Koindu where the borders of Sierra Leone, Liberia, and Guinea meet. In April the rebels opened a second front in the Pujehun and Kenema districts to the south, capturing the border town of Zimmi, then fanning out toward Pujehun town and a military base at Daru. The locations of the attacks seemed ideal if popular support for a revolution was the goal. Opposition to the government simmered in this region where people had never fully accepted the APC. But instead of offering hope for some improvement in the lives of the people, the rebels opened fire on them and helped themselves to their property. Younger villagers were rounded up and forced to join the invaders, who called their movement the Revolutionary United Front.

President Momoh dispatched the bulk of his army to stop the invasion, but his troops were hopelessly unprepared. Apart from token appearances in Congo during 1962, in Persian Gulf I, and with ECOMOG in Liberia, Sierra Leone's army had never fought a war. Combat training was rare; by one count only two such drills had taken place in the previous fourteen years. Weapons were outdated, and much equipment had fallen into disrepair. Still, the government talked of success at the front, claiming the re-capture of several towns.

A KEY FIGURE in the country's defense was Fadugu's most prominent citizen. Deputy Force Commander Achmed B. Thoronka (sometimes spelled Toronka), son of Paramount Chief Alimamy Fana I, had been part of a class of elite recruits brought in to Africanize the former colonial army's officer corps. He graduated from the Mons Officer Cadet School in Aldershot, England, in 1964 then returned home to work his way up from the bailiwick of the army's small signals squadron. Some twenty years later, following Momoh's inauguration as president, Thoronka attained the rank of brigadier, number three in the chain of command behind the president and Force Commander M.S. Tarawallie. A few days after the first rebel attacks, Thoronka traveled north to Conakry as part of a delegation to ask for Guinea's help.

Intervention by Guinean soldiers, those of Sierra Leone's more distant neighbor Nigeria, and a band of anti-Taylor Liberians living in Sierra Leone known as ULIMO (United Liberation Movement of

Liberia for Democracy) appeared to turn the tide. The RUF failed to hold most of the territory it had attacked. A November visitor to Thoronka's office at Freetown's Murray Town Barracks was struck by the lack of a sense of urgency. "They took us by surprise, but we've got them on the run now," he said. Indeed the president himself, in a public address bidding farewell to some of the Guineans, declared the war to be "virtually now over."

That this was not to be was, in part, Thoronka's fault. He and his fellow officers relished the "big man" role as much as the politicians. The diminutive Thoronka—scarcely more than five feet tall and lacking the paunch that usually accompanies success in Sierra Leone—cruised around Freetown in a chauffeur-driven Mercedes Benz and sent his children off to school in London. He had purchased farm land at Newton a few miles east of Freetown, and with help from his brother, Paramount Chief Alimamy Fana II, he acquired more on the outskirts of Fadugu. There he cultivated oil palm and other cash crops with free labor from potential army enlistees.

Every military officer seemed to have an outside enterprise of one kind or another, manned by an assortment of young Sierra Leoneans desperate for the army's steady, though meager salary and monthly bag of rice. Such methods of recruitment seemed unlikely to entice the country's best to join up. Coupled with the politicians' use of the military as a repository for party supporters, it didn't bode success in the prosecution of a war. The army's weakness, indeed its utter corruption, could not be concealed for long.

FOR FADUGU RESIDENTS, nearly 200 miles north of the fighting, life went on as usual. The faceless RUF seemed little more than another negative indicator.

> Life in S. Leone is not as good as it used to be. Things are
> going from bad to worst. With all our diamonds, gold, and
> agricultural produce things are not still good. In fact the rebel
> incursion from Liberia into this country has added salt to injury.
> As for corruption, that is the order of the day. It will take a very

long time before things in the country will improve. When the country's economy is bad, it is bad for everyone, even for those yet unborn.

Business is going on as normal in the midst of high inflationary pressures, continuous devaluation of the Leone (our currency) and other trade barriers.

Umaru Mansaray
Fadugu, Aug. 18, 1991

In spite of all the problems business was better than normal for Umaru and Alie Mansaray. Sales were so strong that the brothers had managed to obtain a used Datsun pickup truck from the United States. Shipped in late 1991 from North Carolina to Guinea and then driven on to Freetown, the vehicle languished for the next several months in the nether world of a customs office driven by bribery.

The truck finally went to Fadugu in mid-February [1992].
Before that, it had already been rumoured that the Gov't. had arrested the van because we were unable to pay the custom duty.
The very day we got to Fadugu everybody was surprised to see it....

We have started to use the truck to sell our goods at Badala on Saturdays. This is 30 miles from Fadugu where an American gold mining company is based. We have gained a lot of customers. This 'mobile shop' idea will be of more help since we are going to increase our sales. It is now in a good running order.

Umaru Mansaray
Fadugu, March 23, 1992

FREETOWN DURING THIS PERIOD seemed as detached from the war as Fadugu. Reports from the front were overwhelmed by talk of a return to multi-party democracy. At the end of March 1991, a few days after the first RUF attacks, the National Constitutional Review Commission, appointed to refurbish APC rule, bowed to public opinion and recommended an end to the one-party state. The president himself embraced the commission's report. If initial rumors were true, that the RUF merely sought an end to the APC's reign, that goal now appeared to be achievable through the ballot box.

On July 2, 1991, parliament voted to amend the country's constitution to allow for multiple parties. The public endorsed the changes during a nationwide referendum at the end of August. Politicians scrambled to regroup as a feeling of liberation swept the country. Several prominent APC members, including former vice-president Salia Jusu-Sheriff and foreign minister Abdul K. Koroma, defected to form new parties. The initial euphoria dimmed with the realization that many all-too-familiar names headed the new political alignment. "New wine in old bottles," *West Africa* soberly called it. Still, the prospect of competition in the race for voters appeared to offer a glimmer of hope that a new government, albeit a retread, would begin to address the country's manifold problems.

In the months that followed, the vectors of war and politics began to converge. While the RUF appeared unable to hold much ground, it also proved elusive. Adopting a hit-and-run approach, the rebels attacked relentlessly, looting and destroying a succession of towns and villages along the southeastern frontier while taking prisoners to be "re-educated" as RUF fighters. The raids disrupted planting and curtailed harvests, which in turn led to shortages in Freetown.

A campaign in April of 1992 to register voters for the as yet unscheduled multi-party elections had to be restricted to northern and western parts of the country untouched by the fighting. Refugees flooded into Guinea in the east and northward in Sierra Leone bringing tales of mass killing, mutilation, and rape. Soldiers at the front complained bitterly of a lack of support. Their officers were said to be enriching themselves with money and materials appropriated for the war.

In the early morning hours of April 29, 1992, shots rang out near President Momoh's residence on Spur Road in the hills of western Freetown. A few hours later, shortly after 8:00 A.M., fighting between factions of the army erupted around State House in the center of town. President Momoh, in a noontime radio address, assured the country that everything was under control. The situation, he said, was caused by a few "malcontents" protesting conditions in the army. An hour later, broadcasting from another radio station, an army captain named Valentine Strasser announced that the Momoh government had been overthrown.

With Force Commander Tarawallie on a visit to North Korea, responsibility for defending the regime fell to his deputy, Achmed Thoronka. A substantial portion of the forces based in Freetown failed to rally behind him, however, and sometime in the early evening, Thoronka and Momoh fled to Guinea. The following day, as it became clear that the coup had succeeded, Captain Strasser went back on the radio to offer a justification.

> Fellow citizens, for over 23 years we have been misruled by an oppressive, corrupt, exploitative and tribalistic bunch of crooks and traitors under the umbrella of the APC government. This regime has perpetuated nepotism, tribalism, gross mismanagement and total collapse of our economic, education, health, transport and communication systems. This regime has brought permanent poverty and a deplorable life for most Sierra Leoneans. This regime has failed us woefully. For Sierra Leone, the past 23 years can only be described as the lost decades. It is all over now.

Most Sierra Leoneans likely agreed with this assessment. Freetown's civilians danced in the streets while soldiers looted the homes and offices of former government officials.

> Well, I was here in Freetown when the coup took place. It was a bad experience that day and the two days which followed. We had to keep indoors throughout. Alie came to Freetown the very day of the coup. So today, we are both trying to go back to Fadugu to see the family. Thieves and looters tried twice to take our vehicle away, but neighbors came to our help. So [the thieves] took the wheel nuts of the right rear wheel away and [also] the tool kit. We are trying to get those nuts today before departure. Datsun Motor Company was totally looted.
>
> Umaru Mansaray
> Freetown, May 4, 1992

Although the coup was said to have originated among the lower ranks, including a private, their mid-level superiors seized control of the movement. The soldiers formed a government called the National Provisional Ruling Council (NPRC) with Captain Strasser as its chairman and the country's head of state. Strasser, most recently, had been serving as paymaster for the battalion based at Makeni. According to his account, he had served with ECOMOG in Liberia, then returned home to fight the invading RUF. He had been severely wounded at the front, he said, and had been hospitalized for several months before his transfer to Makeni. He pledged that the NPRC would bring the rebel war to an end and return the country to "true" multi-party democracy.

As time went on two views of the new military government began to emerge. Those engaged in business activities viewed the soldiers with distrust.

> The coup came at a time when nobody was expecting it. Everyone was going with the belief that coups will never succeed in this country again. But on April 29, 1992, God gave another leader to this country. It was indeed a mistake on the side of the president and his cabinet for failing to provide salary and logistic support for our soldiers at the war front. . . .
>
> We are of course affected because we are forced to sell goods below the cost price. They are only using force everywhere. Soldiers will just come and take away some items without [paying] money. There is no discipline in the army. Most of them are thieves. The check points have increased considerably between Fadugu and Freetown. At any of these check points soldiers demand money. This has created fear in the business sector.
>
> I am glad about one thing and that is the detention of politicians who have wrecked this nation. Accountability is not a key word in anything we do these days.
>
> Umaru Mansaray
> Fadugu, June 10, 1992

Other Sierra Leoneans, those who relied on government salaries, saw a glimmering of better times.

> Our new government seems to be doing well at the moment. There are signs of law and order in the country, as against the former regime where there was no law and order. All the corrupt politicians in the former regime are at Pademba Road prison awaiting trial.
>
> Civil servants and other government employees have received 100% pay rise, though it is still too small. Some teachers have been receiving less than Le3,000.00 [$7] monthly salary, so giving them 100% salary increase brings them to something just around Le6,000.00, which is not enough to buy a bag of rice.... However, we remain optimistic, since it is too early to criticize or recommend, but I firmly believe any government for now is better than the former regime.
>
> A.K. Bangura
> Fadugu, Aug. 25, 1992

The change of government seemed to make little impact at the war front where things continued to go badly. Chairman Strasser offered amnesty to any rebels who disarmed, and he declared his willingness to negotiate with their leaders if a ceasefire could be worked out. In a rare interview conducted in Abidjan, Côte d'Ivoire, RUF leader Foday Sankoh rejected the offer.

Indeed the RUF substantially widened the war in October with attacks on the diamond-producing district of Kono. Government soldiers were said to have been doing a little mining of their own, and the rebels caught them off guard. Thousands of civilians fled on foot as the invaders looted the principal mining town of Koidu.

The attack on Koidu appeared to have been carefully planned. In the preceding months, RUF operatives posing as civilians drifted into town in an effort to assess its defenses. When the time came these advance men directed their comrades to the most strategic targets. The attack also included an element of opportunism, if not downright collusion.

Several sources reported that government troops, still chafing at the lack of support they received despite the recent coup, joined in the spree of looting. In the coming months, such reports would give rise to the term "sobel," soldier-rebel.

> We are now worried about the rebel war in our country. One-fifth of the country is now in rebel hands. We are exposed to attacks at any time since Kono borders Koinadugu District. As for Kono, the rebels have taken it. Don't be surprised to hear that we are refugees in neighboring Guinea. Because of the unstable situation, we have suspended all buyings. We are trying to sell our goods and be on the standby. The future of Sierra Leone is bleak. Rebels have destroyed cacao and coffee and now they have captured the diamond rich Kono. Do you think this land will see peace again?
>
> Umaru Mansaray
> Fadugu, Dec. 12, 1992

Umaru Mansaray

Chapter Six

WAR UP NORTH

The east of Sierra Leone resembled America's wild west. Just as gold sparked the quest for riches on the American frontier, diamonds fostered dreams of instant wealth in modern Sierra Leone. Almost from the moment of their discovery in 1930, the diamonds of Kono District became a powerful lure, attracting peasants and politicians, outsiders and adventurers in pursuit of prosperity through guile or luck. Fadugu's best houses were built from diamond money. Most of the country's other towns and villages could make the same boast.

Sierra Leone's richest diamond fields lie roughly between the Sewa River to the west and the Male River in the east. Belts, or dikes, of kimberlite rock found in Kono, and in an area to the south known as Tongo Field in Kenema District, yielded Sierra Leone's treasure through a centuries-long process of erosion. Rainfall and river flow dislodged chunks of the kimberlite and deposited them over broad areas downstream. The chunks themselves then began to disintegrate, eventually leaving only bits of crystalline carbon, diamonds. These are known as alluvial deposits. Although the potential is there to mine the kimberlite pipes themselves, alluvial deposits are the primary source of diamonds in Sierra Leone.

Early on British colonial authorities managed to keep the diamond fields under relative control. In exchange for a percentage collected as a tax on profits, they granted exclusive rights for the mining and prospecting of diamonds to Sierra Leone Selection Trust (SLST), a subsidiary of De Beers Consolidated Mines of South Africa. De Beers, through a broad network of associated companies, has operated as a near monopoly in the world's diamond markets since the mid-1930s, keeping prices artificially high by purchasing rough gems from all comers while "tailoring supplies to the cutting centres to meet prevailing demand." With the arrival of the 1950s, however, De Beers and the colonial government began to lose control in Sierra Leone. Hundreds at first, then thousands of young men abandoned farms and schools to seek their fortunes in Kono.

The action centered in Koidu, a rowdy squatter town just east of the district headquarters at Sefadu. Koidu's salvage yard of tin shacks, home to the town's countless would-be-but-weren't-yet tycoons, surrounded the far fewer but more substantial dwellings of those who really had struck it rich. At shops in the center of town, Lebanese merchants sold the three essential tools of diamond mining: pick, shovel, and sieve. Each night illicit diggers fanned out on SLST lands to strip away yards of topsoil and sift the underlying gravel where, if luck would have it, a precious stone would be uncovered.

Others didn't bother with the difficult work. Bandits robbed and con men fleeced, altering fortunes in a matter of seconds. Tension rose, and along with it the number of murders. Cross-border trafficking flourished as illicit diggers, fearing arrest if exposed, sold their stones to clandestine buyers who resold them in Monrovia, Antwerp, Beirut, or Tel Aviv.

As Sierra Leone's first African minister of lands, mines, and labor in the colonial government, future president Siaka Stevens helped negotiate an end to the SLST mining monopoly near the end of 1955. In return for 1,570,000 British pounds (approximately $4,380,000 at the time), the company surrendered much of its claim. This allowed the government to open some diamond fields to private, licensed miners—a system it hoped would restore order and reduce smuggling. De Beers, through a new subsidiary called the Diamond Corporation, continued to buy any stone presented.

With the arrival of independence in 1961, Sierra Leone's politicians scrambled for their own piece of the action. Stevens in particular appeared to be attuned to the opportunities, both personal and political, that the presence of diamonds afforded. As a rhetorical populist and leader of the opposition he won broad support in Kono with his declaration that the indigenous people should derive more from the bonanza that lay beneath their feet. Stevens and his All People's Congress won the 1967 elections in part because of overwhelming support from Kono.

Once in power, however, Stevens began to use the country's diamonds for his own benefit. He brazenly intervened in the affairs of a number of chiefdoms in Kono District, imposing his candidates for paramount chief against the wishes of the people. In 1971 Stevens engineered a partial nationalization of SLST with the formation of the National Diamond Mining Company (NDMC) in which the government assumed a fifty-one percent share while SLST retained forty-nine percent. Two years later he introduced Cooperative Contract Mining, a plan that purported to open some NDMC land to local people. In practice the authorities doled out mining plots to political supporters instead, an action that guaranteed illicit digging would continue.

In 1974 the Stevens government ended the exclusive control over the legal purchase of diamonds that De Beers had enjoyed through the Diamond Corporation. Money that flowed into government coffers from taxes on the value of diamond purchases would now depend on the honesty of a handful of new middlemen and the politicians to whom they owed allegiance. This new scheme brought Stevens into a fruitful partnership with the businessman Jamil Said Mohammed.

Jamil, as he is known throughout Sierra Leone, is said to have been born in Port Loko, the son of a Lebanese father and a Sierra Leonean mother. He joined the diamond rush in the 1950s and was jailed by colonial authorities for attempting to smuggle some $30,000 worth of freshly mined stones. With the dawn of independence Jamil rebounded nicely, ingratiating himself with Albert Margai and then Siaka Stevens. Stevens appointed Jamil to the NDMC board of directors and together they served on the board of the Government Diamond Office whose function was to purchase and value diamonds from private diggers.

This shadowy operation abounded in corruption. According to a report compiled by Partnership Africa Canada, a coalition of organizations promoting sustainable development policies, "From a high of over two million carats [one carat equals .2 grams] in 1970, legitimate diamond exports dropped to 595,000 in 1980 and fell to only 48,000 carats in 1988."

Largely because of Lebanese middlemen like Jamil, Sierra Leone's diamonds became a factor in the affairs of the Middle East. When civil war broke out in Lebanon in 1975 diamond money helped finance the Amal Movement led by one Nabih Berry, a friend of Jamil's who was also born in Sierra Leone. In addition, Jamil arranged for the Byblos Bank of Beirut to extend credit to the Stevens regime when other foreign sources began to dry up.

Upon Joseph Momoh's arrival in the presidency, Jamil organized a state visit to Freetown for Palestine Liberation Organization leader Yasir Arafat. But with the new president eager to establish his own political and economic arrangements Jamil's influence waned, all the more so when he was accused of involvement in a 1987 coup plot.

Into the void moved a Russian-born Israeli named Shaptai Kalmanowitch. Kalmanowitch, who was reported to have ties to Israel's military intelligence network, had made his fortune in apartheid-era South Africa, in the "homeland" of Bophuthatswana, as head of LIAT Finance, Trade, and Construction Company. In Sierra Leone LIAT boosted official diamond exports and appeared to be using the earnings to import much needed machinery and equipment. To many observers, however, LIAT's surface activities were merely a cover for circumventing anti-apartheid sanctions. Sierra Leone, it was alleged, was nothing more than a transshipment point for South African diamond exports and imports of strategic goods.

The LIAT-Sierra Leone partnership dissolved in less than two years. Kalmanowitch, it turned out, was wanted in the United States for check fraud. Following his arrest on the US charge in London in 1987, he eventually turned up in Israel, reputedly in custody, in what may have been an effort to conceal his ties to Israel's undercover operations.

Another Israeli entered the scene at this point. Nir Guaz, managing director of the N.R. SCIPA company, came to Freetown with connections to the Israeli government and promises of help to Sierra Leone. In return for a piece of the diamond trade, Guaz rescued the Momoh regime on more than one occasion by financing imports of oil and rice when no other source of funds could be found. But Guaz paid suspiciously high prices for diamonds and his on-the-record exports were low, a combination that led some to believe he was a smuggler, a money-launderer, or both. He too would soon depart.

With this sorry history in mind and their new military rulers exhibiting many of the venal tendencies of the old politicians, many Sierra Leoneans wondered if they would live to see an honest, competent government.

> There are problems in S.L. Business has fallen to its minimum.
> Money circulation has reduced. Workers are being sacked
> everyday. Our leaders continue to smuggle our diamonds and
> gold abroad. Development programmes are geared towards
> the urban areas. The soldiers continue to harass and take
> our property by force. This Gov't. is now doing things they
> overthrew the past regime for. So where is the hope? No hope.
> They are all bunches of thieves. It is the worst Gov't. we have
> ever had. There is one thing common in S.L., the situation will
> never improve....
>
> When I was working in Mongo with K.I.A.D.P. [Koinadugu
> Integrated Agricultural Development Project], I thought one
> could live a more meaningful life if one should set up a strong
> agricultural base. I decided to go to Njala for further studies....
> I came out with the hope of setting up [a farm]. But factors
> beyond my control could not give me the hope I was looking
> for. Land has been the most bottle neck that has prevented us
> from meeting that goal. Now the problem of a road [to available
> land] is also there. The agricultural project will take time to
> establish, especially when we need more time and resources to
> build that road.... What is more discouraging is that Gov't. has
> totally neglected rural development. The rural areas will not

develop without feeder roads. But again the main roads in the country are in a very bad shape. So for Gov't. to think about feeder roads will take a very long time. One thing I keep asking myself is why NGOs, Gov't. and other charitable organizations have failed to support feeder roads?...

My dream of 1989 to set up an agricultural base is still held up by the twin problems of land & road. It is because of this problem that I have decided to go [abroad] for further studies. Because waiting for these problems to be solved will need a long time. I am confident that one day in the distant future things will go through. But if I should go now and read [for a degree] quickly, I will come back to take a more responsible role in society. I have the hope that there is nothing [more] real than agriculture. It is genuine and reliable. But time is running out.

Umaru Mansaray
Fadugu, Oct. 25, 1993

IF SIERRA LEONEANS LIKE UMARU had lost hope and wanted to leave, it is possible to imagine how some who lacked his education and his contacts in America might be tempted by talk of armed revolt. After all, the APC had successfully recruited scores of young and undereducated men as thugs to help keep the party in power. Foday Sankoh tapped the same vein of alienation to build his Revolutionary United Front.

According to Sankoh, he "planned to fight to liberate this country" while in prison for his involvement in the 1971 coup attempt. After his release in 1976 he eventually settled in the southern city of Bo where he started a photography business. Although Sankoh claimed that the RUF was founded in 1982 when he began to organize "study groups" around the country, the movement appears to have evolved from the activities of radical (as seen by the APC regime they opposed) college students. Groups at Fourah Bay College like the Gardeners, whose members were at the forefront of the 1977 demonstrations, the Green Book Study Club (the Green Book being Muammar al-Qaddafi's statement of populist political philosophy), and the Pan-African Union gave voice to student grievances and those of the broader society.

In 1985, following an outbreak of campus violence that spilled down Mount Aureol into Freetown, college administrators expelled a number of the more bellicose students and banned student government. According to Sierra Leonean historian Ibrahim Abdullah, while several of the banished went to Ghana to continue their studies, others began to organize against the government in Freetown itself, and in Bo and Kenema where opposition to the APC was already strong. It was during this period that Foday Sankoh joined one of the loose-knit "cells."

Meanwhile, as Abdullah has pieced it together, some of the Sierra Leonean students in Ghana made connections in Libya and arranged to get military training there. They sent home to Sierra Leone for recruits, among them Foday Sankoh. Once in Libya at the Benghazi training site, Sankoh met two other activists: Abu Kanu, an alumnus of Njala University College, and Rashid Mansaray of Freetown. With help from Liberia's Charles Taylor, the recourse to arms proceeded from this small group.

The RUF attack on Koidu in October of 1992 was a bold attempt to seize the country's wealth. Barring outside intervention, whoever controlled the diamond district would likely win the war. Kono's diamonds had flowed into Liberia for years, but under RUF control, arms would flow into Sierra Leone in return. For the moment, however, the rebels seemed content to attack, loot, and withdraw with captured young men "recruited" to fight for the RUF. Government forces soon re-entered Koidu, a badly battered and nearly empty town.

> Most of our relatives from Kono and Tongo are back home [in Fadugu]. They came empty handed when the rebels drove them. Government does not cater for these returnees and it means their relatives have to do so. So we decided to build a mud house near our swamp at Kasasi in Fadugu. It is nearly completed and some people will have to occupy it soon now that [our main house] #37 Makeni Road is congested.
>
> Umaru Mansaray
> Fadugu, April 2, 1993

◆ ◆ ◆

THE INFLUX OF REFUGEES taxed Fadugu's social resources while giving a boost to its commerce. Even as they complained about the country's business climate, the Mansaray brothers ordered another used pickup from the United States. The truck went into service in June 1993, ferrying passengers from Fadugu to Makeni and Kabala. On Sundays Alie, now the proud father of a son named Mamadu, set up the brothers' market stall in the shade of Fadugu's stately mango tree.

Over at the government primary school, A.K. Bangura had suffered an alarming spell of high blood pressure in November of 1992. The attack triggered a stroke that left him in a coma for two days. Still Bangura laid hopeful plans in spite of his bouts of infirmity. He looked forward to the day when he could return to Petifu, the village of his birth, a hundred or so miles southwest in Temne country.

> I have fully recovered from the stroke I had some time ago, but I am of late experiencing various illnesses like stomach ache, fevers, pains, etc., though they are not very serious. I have just recovered from an acute stomach ache which attacked me some ten days ago. I have undergone a series of medical tests and have been taking treatment. As a result of these incessant attacks of various illnesses, I have not been able to do much as expected in writing my second book, and also my typewriter has still not been properly repaired.
>
> On the other hand, I guess you can still remember my father's garden at home. Well, my father himself has died about some eighteen months ago. I am now the eldest son in the family. Of course, you know I have many children. I have planned to go and develop my father's garden, which is now mine. I intend to increase its size, plant more palm trees and mango trees and some lemon trees, leaving only a small area for pineapples [that once took up almost the entire garden].
>
> I have asked for PL480 loan [a US aid program administered by Sierra Leone] many a time, but my application is always turned down, because I do not have money to bribe the authorities concerned. I am very determined to go ahead with this plan as it will in the very near future help me in taking care

of my children, myself, and even help some other people.... The project itself is expected to start next year between May and June

A.K. Bangura
Fadugu, Nov. 11, 1993.

News from the war front appeared to warrant such optimism. The army claimed to have driven the rebels from several important towns in the south and east. Some of the refugees had even returned to Kono. With the war receding a bit, correspondents from Fadugu concerned themselves with personal affairs.

[You] asked me whether I would leave my job to become a complete farmer and talked about how the Kasunko people will feel for losing me. In the first instance, I love my job and love the Kasunko people, but the reason behind my plans is several fold ... (a) I have many children, (b) I am nearing my retirement age, my salary is meagre and sordid, my last daughter is just seven years old and most of my children will still be in school for the next 8 to 9 years. If I do not invest my money that way [in farming], I will not be able to take care of them in the future. The love I have for the job, the people of Kasunko and Koinadugu District in general should not lead me to not be able to take care of myself, my children, dependants and other relatives in the future. I hope my points are clear to you....

My son is now in class VI, and is to go to secondary school next year. He said he will write you when he has money to buy an air mail [aerogramme]. That may be in four years time, because each time he has money he buys cakes, bananas, oranges, etc. He only talks of writing you when he does not have money. Please expect a letter from him when there are no cakes, bananas, oranges, etc. in the whole of Fadugu town.

A.K. Bangura
Fadugu, March 11, 1994

The Mansarays ordered another truck, their third, a four-wheel drive to take their mobile market to remote areas. Alie's wife Salimatu bore a second son, Saraio. And brother Umaru prepared for the end of his bachelorhood.

> I have finally met the woman I would like to marry. She is [Mabinty] the step-daughter of Alhaji Brima Fofana, the man who gave us lodging in Madina on our way to look at the land at Kamathanta. She is 23 and went to school in Freetown. It is nearly a year since she went to spend her time with me in Fadugu.
>
> She applied for the state registered nursing course at the National School of Nursing and has already been short listed for an interview in July. If she is accepted she will have to begin the program in October 1994, a three year course. In the light of this I will have to "put kola" for her on June 15. This is a ceremony that means the beginning of marriage. It will involve all the customs and traditions of a union in an African setting
>
> Umaru Mansaray
> Fadugu, May 27, 1994.

LIFE IN FADUGU seemed nearly normal, but in Freetown the NPRC government struggled to find its footing. The military rulers faced two principal demands: end the war and redress the evils of the civilians they had thrown out. It was unclear if they possessed the will or the means to do either. Although their rhetoric inspired hope, the soldiers flaunted their authority. They ordered new cars for themselves and moved into mansions confiscated from the politicians. Rumors circulated that they too were smuggling diamonds. Critics in the press were hauled to Criminal Investigations Department headquarters for questioning.

Cosmetic activities, the cleaning of Freetown and commissions of inquiry into the ill-gotten gains of the politicians diverted people's attention for much of 1992. The regime's pledge to return the country to civilian rule received some impetus that same year with the appointment of an advisory council to work out the details. Negotiations for financial help from the International Monetary Fund appeared to be making progress. But 1992 ended badly when the regime, under cover of an alleged coup attempt, executed twenty-nine opponents. The image of this group being lined up and shot after a summary trial before a secret tribunal produced a fusillade of condemnation from Western nations whose good will the regime sorely needed.

Those Western nations had, up to this point, shown little interest in helping the government fight the RUF. Nigeria, whose intervention should logically have drawn support, was given the cold shoulder by the West because of its human rights abuses and suspension of democracy at home. United Nations agencies under Western control, the IMF and World Bank, did eventually come through with loans. Sierra Leone had agreed to follow the "structural adjustment" formula through cuts in the number of government employees, reductions in its budget deficit, sale of state-owned enterprises, and stabilization of the leone. By 1994 the NPRC was earning praise from the international financial establishment while the people, whose impoverishment the "reforms" had exacerbated, grew increasingly angry.

> Teachers both primary and secondary schools in the whole of the country will go to an indefinite strike on Wednesday 26 Oct., because of poor working conditions. You couldn't believe this … our August salary has still not been paid, and besides the highest paid teacher gets something around Le28,000.00 [$48] and Le30,000.00, while others receive less than Le20,000.00 per month. This is indeed a big problem. There is no money in the country at all. We have to do all sorts of odd jobs to enable us to get something to feed our families. I will definitely quit the job soon and concentrate in my garden work
>
> A.K. Bangura
> Fadugu, Oct. 24, 1994.

The army itself reflected the heightened tension. Captain S.A.J. Musa, deputy to NPRC chairman Valentine Strasser, was sent on leave to London in the middle of 1993 for dissenting from government policy. Musa and another army captain were later accused of planning a coup. Many senior officers appeared reluctant to carry out orders from their juniors who constituted the NPRC government. Thirteen of the recalcitrant seniors were sacked in 1994, but the effect was to weaken a fighting force whose resolve was already suspect.

Optimistic reports from the front throughout 1993 had the rebels retreating in disarray. Defectors from the RUF told of disagreements within the leadership in 1992 that resulted in the executions of two of the movement's founders, Abu Kanu and Rashid Mansaray. RUF supply lines were disrupted and retreat into Liberia blocked by the anti-Taylor soldiers of ULIMO (United Liberation Movement of Liberia for Democracy), who had fought the RUF inside Sierra Leone for a time before moving across the border to occupy parts of northwestern Liberia.

By 1994, however, the RUF had retaken the initiative. Kailahun and Kenema Districts were attacked with renewed ferocity. In an apparent attempt to gain international attention, the rebels ambushed a convoy led by foreign missionaries in March, murdering an Irish priest and a Dutch family of three. The following month they raided villages near the important Northern Province town of Magburaka.

> I would by now have gone [to my home village of Petifu] for my garden work, but the rebel activity extended to the Northern Province and went very close to our chiefdom, and many people had to flee to other parts of the country for safety. Not too long ago … people in that area started returning after the rebel attack in that area was mercilessly repelled by a combined force of our soldiers and local hunters. The place is now safe and life has returned to normal.
>
> A.K. Bangura
> Fadugu, June 29, 1994

Anthropologist Paul Richards once suggested that perhaps the RUF committed mayhem with clear intent. Foday Sankoh, being a photographer, may have been "carefully compiling a picture designed to project the aspirations of his movement through deeds rather than words."

If so, it was a picture that made the former APC government, whose corrupt rule had given rise to the RUF, look downright benevolent by comparison.

Another observer, journalist Bill Berkeley, has likened (rightly, for the most part) Africa's warring factions to the families of organized crime. In Sierra Leone Siaka Stevens and, with less success, Joseph Momoh played the godfather. As for the RUF, it was impossible to know the mind of its leader or to what ends a Sankoh administration might work. Still, there was little to suggest that once in power the rebels would break the mold. This was no "tribal" conflict. The RUF was a pastiche of volunteers and conscripts of every stripe bent not on ethnic retribution but on supplanting the reigning mafia. The murder of local elders, mutilation of captives, and wanton destruction of villages belied Sankoh's "revolutionary" rhetoric. A sense of gloom weighed on the country, even far from the fighting.

> My engagement to Binty Fofana ended in a wedding on the 13th July 1994 according to Mandingo custom. Mr. A.K. Bangura was chairman of the occasion. Binty has finally joined me at the new house along Kasasi road.
>
> My plans to go to the U.S.A. will not change as conditions continue to worsen. Every day, every week, and every month, one hears of one town or village burning under rebel attack, bandits, run-away soldiers, etc. These kinds of behavior are neither justified politically or religiously. Sales have also dropped because people's demand has decreased due to an increase in poverty.
>
> Umaru Mansaray
> Fadugu, July 29, 1994

The rebels' resurgence stemmed, in part, from their growing aura of invincibility. RUF leaders were reported to be using Rambo videos to inspire new conscripts. Local marijuana (*diamba*) and imported cocaine braced the troops for battle. They were lightly armed—carrying only Kalashnikov AK-47 assault rifles, mortars, and rocket propelled grenades for the most part—and therefore highly mobile. The rebels seemed especially adept at reconnaissance, which helped their attacks achieve maximum surprise.

There was also growing evidence that the rebels enjoyed the assistance of renegade members of the Sierra Leone army. The military government expanded the army, a process begun by the Momoh administration, by hurriedly arming and haphazardly training recruits from among the same marginal elements of society that fought for the RUF. Stories of soldiers mining diamonds and selling supplies to the RUF circulated widely. Rebels occasionally attacked wearing Sierra Leone army uniforms, while some of the raids attributed to the RUF were staged by government soldiers. The latter group were the "sobels," soldier-rebels who bore allegiance to neither side.

For help the government enlisted members of the *Tamaboroh* society, a multi-ethnic group of hunters from the northern Koinadugu District who were thought to possess supernatural powers. Other areas of the country began to organize self-defense forces—most prominently the Mende people's *Kamajo* hunters—as the army's trustworthiness rapidly diminished.

Despite such reinforcements government troops continued to perform poorly. Most of the fighting stayed south and east, but rebels also made forays to the north. Following their attacks near Magburaka in April 1994—which may actually have been staged by sobels—rebel bands moved into Koinadugu District. They made no attempt to hold territory, preferring instead to loot and "recruit" while demonstrating that they could strike almost anywhere. In October, after several raids on outlying villages, the district headquarters town of Kabala, and with it Fadugu, looked dangerously vulnerable.

> Rebels of the R.U.F. attacked Kabala on the 7 November 94, at
> about 5:05 P.M. There was no security, in other words, there
> was very little or no resistance from any of our armed forces,
> and so a lot of destruction took place. About 95 houses were set
> ablaze, property worth millions of leones was looted and about

10 people mostly civilians including two S.S.D. [Special Security Division] personnel officers were killed.

On the very day of the attack, almost everybody left Fadugu and went into hiding or seeking refuge for fear of the same rebel attack. In all only about 8 people were in the town that day including one woman. All the villages along the Kabala–Makeni road were forced to move....

Hannah Bangura, my [seven-year-old] daughter, walked 25 miles on foot to a village called Kasandikoro without her mother or me. There was a kind of at random running. She took three days in the village before we could know her whereabouts. However, everything appears to be calm now, and all members of my family are with me. Schools have reopened in Kasunko Chiefdom, but none in Kabala.

A.K. Bangura
Fadugu, Dec. 14, 1994

Our business has now come to standstill with some of our market centres destroyed. In that event we lost our customers some of whom are dead now. Of all our market centres, Badala which is 35 miles from Fadugu was most prominent. It is there that we had our highest sales a minimum of Le600,000.00 (US$1,000) every week. Now that that village is almost destroyed by rebels when they attacked Kabala we don't see an immediate market for our goods. There is also fear of rebels revisiting Kabala, who knows Fadugu, which is just a stone throw away.

Umaru Mansaray
Fadugu, Dec. 2, 1994

Beyond the ruinous destruction of property, the Kabala attack inflicted heavy psychological damage. The Sierra Leone army, at best, had abandoned the fight. Many accused the soldiers of collaborating with the rebels. The Tamaboroh hunters, once imagined to be superhuman, saw their leader, Dembaso Samura, singled out and brutally murdered. Who among the common people could feel secure?

I have not been coming to Freetown since I last talked with you on the telephone just after the rebels attacked Kabala and our subsequent return to Fadugu. Well, for the past months the rebels have made passenger vehicles their target. A lot of people have lost their lives along the Makeni–Freetown and Bo–Freetown roads. At last I decided to come to [Free]town.

Binty gave birth to a baby boy and both of them are doing fine. The baby is named after my father, Mohamed. On March 21, he will be 3 months old....

As of now our business has come to standstill. The country is on the verge of collapse. The R.U.F. rebels have made civilians their target of late. I am even afraid for my life and others. There is always rumors that they will come to Fadugu. And if they come we will be their target. We are not safe any longer. Only God will help.

Umaru Mansaray
Freetown, Feb. 9, 1995

Thor "Mammy Thor" Konteh

Chapter Seven

ELECTIONS BEFORE PEACE

The sack of Kabala marked a turning point in Sierra Leone's war. That such an obvious target could so easily be overrun confirmed the army's confusion. Emboldened by the lack of resistance, RUF rebels stepped up the pace of their attacks.

In the middle of January 1995, as harmattan winds blew dry and hot, the rebels raided Mobimbi and Mokanji, neighboring towns in the southwest where bauxite and rutile were mined. Bauxite, the raw material of aluminum, and rutile (titanium dioxide), used in making paint, ranked just below diamonds in importance to the country's economy. Now, as the foreign firms that operated the mines evacuated their personnel, the government would lose this vital source of income.

Less than a week later, rebels moved north within sight of Guinea for a raid on the strategic town of Kambia. Dozens of young men were captured and forced to join their attackers. Houses were looted and a police station burned while thousands of townspeople fled across the border. The RUF suddenly appeared unstoppable.

> The whole country is not secure when one looks at the speed at which the rebels [are] killing innocent civilians and the mass destruction of property. In fact, to come to F/town these days, you have to risk your life. The rebels have made everything their target, passenger vehicles, innocent civilians, property, mining companies, farms, animals, and everything. Today we are at the mercy of 'monsters'. We don't know when this war will actually

end. It will take many years before we could [return to] the
1992 standard which we S. Leoneans thought was the worst.

Umaru Mansaray
Fadugu, March 25, 1995

EVEN AS THEY TERRORIZED most Sierra Leoneans the latest attacks
aimed for a wider audience. Rebels abducted two workers from the
British aid organization Voluntary Service Overseas (VSO) during the
Kabala raid. Eight foreign (British, German, and Swiss) employees of
the bauxite and rutile mines were captured in those attacks. And in
Kambia the rebels seized seven Roman Catholic nuns, six Italians and
one from Brazil.

Up to this point RUF leader Foday Sankoh had failed to emulate
his ally Charles Taylor in the public relations department. Throughout
his fight for power in Liberia Taylor had skillfully used a satellite telephone to contact international news organizations—primarily the
BBC—to get his message out. Sankoh, on the other hand, remained
strangely inaccessible, so much so that many Sierra Leoneans doubted
his existence.

After the kidnapping of the two VSO workers, however, Sankoh
began to surface. In a December 1994 call to the BBC he rejected the
Sierra Leone government's offer of a ceasefire and RUF participation in
returning the country to democracy. He threatened instead to hold the
hostages until Britain stopped supplying arms to government troops.
In a subsequent radio broadcast in Sierra Leone, Sankoh linked the
fate of the hostages to that of a Sierra Leone army officer who had been
sentenced to death by a military tribunal for selling army supplies to
the RUF.

The public relations effort continued near the end of January 1995
when another Sankoh, RUF foreign relations officer Alimamy Bakarr
Sankoh, gave an interview to a Nigerian free-lance journalist in Abidjan.
This Sankoh claimed that the hostages were being held for their own
protection. National reconciliation, he said, could not be achieved un-

til the foreign forces—most prominently Nigerian and Guinean—assisting the government were withdrawn.

In a follow-up letter to *West Africa* magazine Alimamy Sankoh denied that the RUF was a military force: "It is the power of the mass of the Sierra Leonean people united in their legitimate struggle to rid themselves of the bondage of black neo-colonialism." In what appeared to be a reference to the RUF's penchant for attacking civilians, Sankoh claimed a "commitment to the rule of law and respect for human rights" and said the RUF "has surely punished all acts of abuse which have been brought to its attention."

Later in the year, in answer to the barrage of condemnation that branded it a collection of butchers and looters with no plan for improving the country, the RUF issued a lengthy manifesto entitled "Footpaths to Democracy." This declaration was based on a so-called "Basic Document" of the RUF that, according to historian Ibrahim Abdullah, was actually written by the Sierra Leonean students in exile in Ghana before Foday Sankoh's rebel movement was born. Sankoh and his cohorts expropriated the mishmash of Mao, Qaddafi, and Amilcar Cabral and altered it to suit their purposes.

"We are democrats," the new document declared, "and we stand for progress through work and happiness." It restated the RUF indictment of the former APC government and derided the current military regime as "the rebel NPRC" and "APC watchdogs." One of the more constructive sections spoke of the "civil society" being "allowed to determine its own future through a representative sovereign national conference leading to a people's constituent assembly which in turn would form a government of national unity." More nebulous passages called for the overhaul of local government "so that everybody participates fully and actively in the decision making and implementing processes according to their ability"; for people to "empower themselves in order to harness their resources"; for "a national democratic revolution—involving the total mobilization of all progressive forces"; and for "a cultural revolution whose main objective will be the liberation of our minds to instill in everyone of us a high sense of African patriotism."

In action, even as they released the foreign hostages without apparent reciprocity, the rebels that would empower the people of Sierra Leone made war on them instead.

> My garden work has received a serious set-back. Rebels of the R.U.F. attacked my home village of Petifu some time in February this year and caused a lot of damage on life and property. Everybody in the village fled into the bush to escape the killings. The two men who have been taking care of the garden have also fled into the bush, and their whereabouts are still unknown. I hope to visit there at the end of this month to see if I can resume work in May or June.
>
> I managed to buy an old pick axe and a mattock out of the money you sent me, and I have also deposited a small amount for nursed oil palm trees. To be candid, no serious work can take place in the country under this state of chaos and anarchy. Until this senseless war comes to a complete end, the whole country will always be in a state of terror....
>
> The rebels are only a few miles to the capital Freetown, so we are all waiting to see if they can enter and take over government. Probably that will bring about the end of the war.
>
> A.K. Bangura
> Fadugu, April 12, 1995

An RUF unit had managed to establish a base camp in the Malal Hills behind the old iron mining town of Lunsar. From there the rebels staged their raid on A.K. Bangura's ancestral home and the kidnapping of the nuns at Kambia. With the scent of success in the wind, the rebels began to advance on Freetown. In April they captured Songo, some twenty miles from the capital, in effect cutting the city off from the rest of the country. As the rebels moved on Waterloo, the last major target before Freetown itself, government forces mounted a fierce defense. Reinforced by fresh troops from Guinea and Nigeria, the army halted the rebel advance. A nervous capital relaxed for the moment, but it was clear that if the government wanted to vanquish the RUF more help would be required.

The NPRC had already arranged for a private firm called Gurkha Security Guards to come to Sierra Leone to help train the army. This outfit, nearly five dozen mercenaries from the Gurkha ethnic group of Nepal who had previously served in the British army, operated from Camp Charlie, a military base near Mile 91 on the road from Freetown to Bo. The Gurkhas and their American leader, Robert MacKenzie, had joined in an end-of-February assault on the nearby RUF base in the Malal Hills in what appeared to be an attempt to free the hostage nuns. MacKenzie and Major Abubakar Tarawallie, the aide-de-camp to NPRC chairman Valentine Strasser, were both killed, and the raid ended in failure. Soon afterward the Gurkhas went home.

To replace them, the NPRC hired another "private security" force based in South Africa called Executive Outcomes (EO). The first of nearly 200 Executive Outcomes soldiers, former enforcers of apartheid and de-stabilizers of Angola and Mozambique, began to arrive in Freetown in May to train and fight alongside members of Sierra Leone's army. EO's black soldiers and their white officers were reported to be earning salaries that ranged from $2000 to $7000 per month drawn from an over-all fee of $1.8 million per month that the cash-poor NPRC had agreed to.

Executive Outcomes brought to the war an expertise, albeit of unsavory origins, and a powerful arsenal, including Russian-built helicopter gunships, two elements Sierra Leone's army sorely lacked. A combined force of EO and Sierra Leonean soldiers rapidly evicted the RUF from much of the territory near Freetown. By June they had taken control of the diamond fields and established a base at Koidu. Soon afterward the NPRC granted a twenty-five-year mining concession to Branch Energy, a company with close ties to Executive Outcomes. Diamond money would flow again, into South African pockets. Nevertheless, Executive Outcomes brought a heightened degree of security, especially in the larger towns where pro-government forces generally based themselves. For that most residents gave thanks.

In the difficult-to-monitor countryside, however, the RUF continued to be a dangerous and increasingly brutal menace. Summarizing the war to date, *West Africa* reported that "scores of citizens have had their heads and hands cut off, and the severed parts dumped in mass graves or displayed at roadblocks across the country. More than 300 villages are depopulated, and have ceased to exist in any meaningful sense." In August, at the height of the rainy season when the RUF was generally less active, the rebels ambushed a convoy of some seventy vehicles carrying food and medicine along the main highway leading from Freetown to Bo. Despite the presence of an armed escort that included a helicopter gunship, dozens of people were killed and many of the vehicles destroyed. Within a few days, A.K. Bangura's ancestral village, located near the convoy attack, was raided for the third time.

> There are fourteen people in my [Fadugu] house, including some of my distant relatives who ran away from the war in my village.
>
> It is now more than 6 months since we stopped talking about our staple food rice. We eat whatever comes our way for the day.
>
> If it were not for this senseless rebel war, I would have preferred going home than to find myself in such a disgraceful and humiliating condition. Staying at home on my garden work and doing some other agricultural piece of work is better than working for government without pay.
>
> I some time hesitate or [am] ashamed to write you, because each time I write I tell you new problems, but since you are my friend and the problems are not my own making, I therefore have no alternative but to let you know. I know you also have other problems and you cannot solve all of them at the same time.
>
> To be frank indeed, as far [as] Sierra Leone is concerned, the problem of the ordinary Sierra Leonean cannot be solved within the next twenty to thirty years.
>
> A.K. Bangura
> Fadugu, Nov. 27, 1995

◆ ◆ ◆

IN HIS APRIL 1992 address to the nation confirming the coup d'etat that dethroned President Momoh and the APC, chairman of the NPRC, Valentine Strasser, had committed his regime "to sincerely pursue the process of returning our country to true multi-party democracy." Given the military's record in Africa, more than a few Sierra Leoneans heard this pledge through skeptical ears. Nevertheless, the NPRC appointed a National Advisory Council in December of 1992 to map the country's return to civilian rule.

The nineteen-member council, drawn from diverse segments of the country's elite, took its work seriously. One year later the council chairman, a veteran of some twenty years at the United Nations Development Programme named Ahmad Tejan Kabbah, presented a 170-page "working document" that would form the basis for a new constitution. The event opened a four-month period of public debate after which a final draft would be prepared.

In January 1994 the NPRC announced that another Sierra Leonean with long experience at the UN, under-secretary for political affairs James Jonah, would be returning home to head the newly established Interim National Electoral Commission. In thirty years at the UN Jonah had undertaken a broad range of assignments including a period as head of the UN's global election monitoring. His qualifications appeared to be impeccable; and he forswore any political ambitions. In spite of the country's profound disarray, the movement to restore constitutional democracy in Sierra Leone had begun to pick up steam.

In October, a month before RUF rebels overran Kabala, Kabbah and his National Advisory Council presented their new draft constitution to Chairman Strasser. It turned out to be an updated version of the former constitution, which had been amended in 1991 to bring an end to one-party rule. Those changes had already been approved in a nationwide referendum during the Momoh regime. After much study and debate the National Advisory Council had added its own modifications and the NPRC accepted this draft as the foundation for Sierra Leone's coming second republic.

Then in June of 1995, as Executive Outcomes scattered the RUF rebels, the NPRC lifted its ban on party politics. Apart from a tainted fifty-seven former APC regulars who were barred from participation, the rest of the country's politicians rushed to re-organize themselves. Seventeen parties initially registered with the electoral commission, including remnants of the APC and the old Sierra Leone People's Party that had led the country at independence. Despite an invitation from the electoral commission, the RUF made no attempt to join the political process.

Public opinion seemed to favor the return of party politics; at least it promised an end to rule by the unpopular soldiers. But there was also a body of dissenters that felt no proper elections could be held in the middle of a war. A movement calling itself the Peace Before Election Campaign, headed by radio broadcaster and newspaper editor Hilton Fyle, proposed that an "interim peoples assembly" be convened to select an interim administration, including RUF representatives, to govern for three years of "national healing." This proposal failed to produce a ground swell of support. The government held its own National Consultative Conference instead, a 154-strong cross section of society assembled in August at the beach-front Bintumani Hotel. Conference delegates voted overwhelmingly to proceed with elections for president and parliament to be held simultaneously the following February.

One new wrinkle that emerged from the Bintumani conference was proportional voting. Under previous civilian governments the country had been divided into geographical constituencies, each of which would elect a representative to sit in parliament. Now, with the war dragging on and some constituencies at the mercy of the RUF, it was decided to adopt James Jonah's suggestion to allocate the sixty-eight ordinary seats in parliament to the parties in proportion to the number of votes each received. As before, twelve additional seats would go to paramount chiefs, one elected from each of the country's administrative districts.

◆   ◆   ◆

ELECTIONS WOULD BRING an end to military rule but not an end to the war. While the politicians jockeyed for power, the people struggled to survive. A.K. Bangura, the Mansaray brothers, and most of their neighbors remained in Fadugu, albeit with much trepidation. Following the attack on Kabala, a company of Nigerian soldiers had garrisoned Fadugu, lodging in rooms around the town and mustering at the chiefdom court. The Nigerians added a semblance of security even as their presence invited retribution.

> The country continues to sink economically. The exchange rate now is Le1100.00 to a dollar. Prices continue to rise. The standard of living continues to drop drastically. The war continues to damage the country further. While innocent people are dying from bullets from the R.U.F. rebels, others are dying from hunger and malnutrition.
>
> In Fadugu we are dying from talk of rebels visiting there. Our country is damaged for good....
>
> From this moment to the time when this country could have been rehabilitated is called the 'black period.' It is during this period I want to leave S. Leone to study abroad. Because during this period every effort will be frustrated. I only hope I will secure the US visa the next time I appear.
>
> Umaru Mansaray
> Fadugu, Dec. 5, 1995

At the same time as he maneuvered to get out of the country, Umaru, and his brother Alie, labored to maintain the last remnants of their business. To the north, the brothers' main source of sales, the Saturday market at Badala, had evaporated when the RUF burned most of the town around the time of its attack on Kabala. To the south, rebel ambushes along the road from Makeni to Freetown made a buying trip to the capital a dangerous gamble. As a result, the Mansarays' trucks stuck to the Kabala–Fadugu–Makeni route where they transported the brave and the desperate to increasingly uncertain fates.

On the outskirts of town, at the government primary school, A.K. Bangura grappled with the effects of high blood pressure and no salary, afflictions no doubt related. A mysterious house fire destroyed many of the family's belongings in February 1995, although timely action by neighbors saved the structure itself. In August, as the new school year began, the needs of Bangura's several children, two of whom required fees for secondary school promotional exams, strained the family's dwindling resources. "There is no money in the country," Bangura wrote at the time, "so it will be a kind of magic to be able to take care of these problems in a state like our kind."

Some of that magic still managed to produce a buli of fresh palm wine nearly every afternoon. At the *barrie* beside his house, a small area enclosed with palm fronds, Bangura and friends argued politics and exchanged gossip in a daily gettogether that usually lightened up as the palm wine buli emptied. Inevitably, their talk would turn to the war and the deteriorating conditions it had imposed on them.

Fadugu's people, nearly all of whom used to grow rice, stayed away from their swamps for fear of rebel attack. Some, in desperation, had eaten their seeds, making another planting impossible. Bellies once used to the sweet taste of rice now had to make do with cassava, beans, millet, and potatoes, which could be grown in small plots closer to home. Most people still raised chickens to eat, and many also kept goats. One of the butchers occasionally brought a cow to market, but with cash in short supply the beef was harder to sell.

For some of the town's more wealthy residents the matter of livestock was one not of food, but finance. Several owned cows as a hedge against inflation. No matter what happened to the unstable leone, cows maintained their value. Even the Mansaray brothers had begun to accumulate a few head, minded in the bush by a cousin. Others kept large herds looked after by Fulas in *waris* (corrals) far from town. Should one sell to prevent their slaughter by rebels and hope inflation wouldn't wreak the same result?

War presented a stream of dilemmas, and yet the people of Fadugu tried to maintain the routine. Parents sent their children to school with hope that a book education would be of value again one day. Teachers continued to teach even as their salaries fell further and further in arrears. Sunday market took place as before, although fear curtailed attendance and sales. Daring truckers kept the tanks at Mammy Thor's petrol station from running dry. Thor herself carried on at her kiosk, selling the bare essentials. As worrisome as it was to stay, there was no better place to go.

THE RUF HAD BEEN largely confined to the bush following the engagement of Executive Outcomes. But there the rebels were in their element, and they skillfully employed its cover. Rebel ambushes disrupted the supply of food and other goods, forcing more and more people to seek relief in refugee camps. Each raid produced new conscripts for the rebels, who used them chiefly as slave labor to bear supplies to the scene of the next attack and to carry the booty back to base.

In October of 1995—in a series of vicious attacks reminiscent of the odious reign of Belgium's King Leopold II, whose agents in Congo chopped off the hands of Africans who failed to harvest their quota of rubber—RUF rebels severed the hands of scores of women between Bo and Moyamba as a warning to cease the rice harvest. *West Africa* reported that "young men who refused to join the RUF had their hands cut off and their Achilles tendons severed."

In the middle of December, the French aid organization, Médecins Sans Frontières (doctors without borders) placed a full-page advertisement in London's *Daily Telegraph* whose chilling headline aimed to arouse the international community: "They're ripping out tongues, gouging eyes and hacking off hands. Christmas in Sierra Leone."

The atrocities seemed to signal the rebels' growing desperation. From the start, their penchant for attacking civilians had alienated the very people who might well have rallied to their cause. As former foreign minister Abdul Koroma, paraphrasing Mao, has written, "By unleashing on the civilian population in the countryside, a show of enormous violence, they violated a classic guerrilla dictum of 'having the people serve as the sea in which the fish can swim.'" Now, with Executive

Outcomes raiding their strongholds and the prospect of elections to end the army's rule, the rebels found themselves militarily and politically isolated.

As election fever began to mount in the new year 1996, the government delivered a shock. The Supreme Military Council of the NPRC voted to remove its chairman, Captain Valentine Strasser, from power. The soldiers appointed Strasser's deputy, Brigadier Julius Maada Bio, as the new NPRC chairman and head of state. A spokesman claimed that Strasser had attempted to "force the NPRC to make some major legislative changes in the electoral laws of this country and start machinations to ensure that he is installed as the next president."

Contrary rumors had it that Strasser supported the return to civilian rule while Bio wanted to keep the soldiers in power. Whatever the case, the new chairman affirmed the government's intention to hold elections, now scheduled for February 26. "Our commitment to restore this country to democratic civilian rule is irreversible," he said in an address to the nation.

Bio also reached out to the RUF: "To you, Corporal Foday Sankoh, the message from my government is that we are prepared to meet with you anywhere, at any time and without preconditions." He offered amnesty for the rebels and appealed to the international community for help in the search for peace.

Soon afterward, Bio and Sankoh held a series of conversations via radio, during which they set a date for face to face talks. The RUF opposed holding the elections, however, and Bio and his NPRC colleagues appeared to be wavering. Peace before elections talk began to revive. In an effort to determine if such a change in direction had support, Bio reconvened the National Consultative Conference on February 12. Conference delegates voted overwhelmingly to proceed with the elections, and the NPRC pledged to honor their preference.

Elections commission chairman James Jonah announced that over 1.6 million Sierra Leoneans had been registered, some sixty percent of those believed to be eligible. The list of parties had dwindled somewhat; former powers, the APC and SLPP, would contest with eleven new formations headed mostly by very old names. The People's National Convention (PNC) included more prominent APC politicos than the current APC itself. Abass Bundu, a former minister in the Stevens government, later executive secretary of ECOWAS, headed the People's Progressive Party. Octogenarian John Karefa-Smart, Sierra Leone's external affairs minister at independence, returned from a long exile in the United States to head the United National People's Party (UNPP). The recent chairman of the advisory council that had updated the constitution, Ahmad Tejan Kabbah, led the SLPP.

Despite Foday Sankoh's agreement to begin peace talks, his rebels emerged from the bush to launch a series of raids aimed at disrupting the vote. Pendembu in the east was partially destroyed in early February, and northern towns, Port Loko, Makeni, and Kambia, were also hit. Security concerns limited campaigning and impeded the distribution of ballot boxes.

Voting day, February 26, began with gunshots. Rebel attacks prevented polling stations from being set up in the northern districts of Tonkolili and Kambia. In the south, Pujehun town was unable to vote, although Bo and Kenema did. Voting continued into the following day to insure that everyone who wanted to, and was willing to take the risk, could cast a ballot. Outside observers called the exercise the best that could be done in the circumstances.

Just under fifty percent of the registered voters managed to participate. Five parties, led by the SLPP and UNPP, received more than five percent of the vote, the threshold for winning seats in parliament. The widely detested APC squeaked in with a little less than six percent, while its clone, the PNC, was shut out. As in past elections, the results broke down along regional, and therefore ethnic, lines. The south and east, largely populated by Mendes, voted overwhelmingly for the SLPP. Northern voters split among the several parties with origins in the north.

Kabbah led the voting for president, gaining nearly thirty-six percent. Karefa-Smart took second with twenty-two. Since the constitution required a new president to be elected with at least fifty-five percent of the vote, Kabbah and Karefa-Smart, two men who had been out of the country for many years and were thought to have little or no political following, would face each other in a runoff. This outcome appeared to be a clear indication of just how ready Sierra Leoneans were to cast off the old guard, which had brought the country to ruin.

While the people digested the election results, representatives of the NPRC government and the RUF rebels finally met face to face. Talks held in Abidjan on February 28 established a semblance of rapport, and both sides agreed to meet again. Still, the rebels refused to sanction the elections.

The runoff proceeded on March 15 with fewer disruptions this time. Kabbah defeated Karefa-Smart with fifty-nine percent of the vote. Soon afterward Bio announced his acceptance of an RUF offer to cease fire unconditionally for two months. On March 25, Bio traveled to Côte d'Ivoire to meet Sankoh for the first time. At Yamoussoukro, the Ivoirean capital, the two leaders agreed to extend the ceasefire and committed each side to further talks. Four days later, Alhaji Ahmad Tejan Kabbah was sworn in as Sierra Leone's new president.

> For now, our internal mail system is better, because of the two months ceasefire announced by the R.U.F. Almost all the major motor roads are clear. I couldn't have definitely written you before now....
>
> Last year, most families, especially those in the rebel occupied areas, lived on raw fruits, leaves, and some even ate lizards and other insects. My family and myself ate certain food which we've never eaten before. Most people who were in those conditions have died, but thank God, we are still alive.
>
> The military government of Maada Bio deleted my name from salary payment vouchers for 8 good months, and when it reappeared in January, I was only paid for that month, January. And in the February salary payment voucher, again my name was deleted. I have definitely decided to quit the job, but the country is not all that safe yet, so I cannot do that....

You have been hearing about Sierra Leonean refugees and displaced people in Guinea and Liberia, that is those who escaped the fighting. But those of us who were not able to escape the fighting remained as refugees and displaced people in our very country and homes, because there was nothing to eat, drink or even clothe ourselves.

It might interest you to know that the R.U.F. rebels have a kind of permanent base or settlement in [Petifu] our [ancestral] home town, this means that all the civilians have either run away or escaped. My brothers and sisters do not know my whereabouts, nor do I know their whereabouts. We only hope that the present ceasefire declared by the R.U.F. will be a lasting one. Probably by next year things would have come completely under control.

We have at last got a civilian government, though it is not the party that I am supporting [that] won the elections. But we hope that that will bring peace and prosperity. I am a strong supporter of UNPP, the party of Dr. John Karefa-Smart. The election was rigged in favour of S.L.P.P.

I hope you will find time to visit us this year. My family and myself are eager to see you.

A.K. Bangura
Fadugu, April 8, 1996

President Kabbah picked up the negotiations with Foday Sankoh where Chairman Bio had left them. The president and the rebel leader met in Yamoussoukro on April 23 where they affirmed their commitment to making peace. Committees of aides were set up to work out the details. In the interim, both parties would refrain from combat. Sierra Leoneans continued to suffer the painful deprivations five years of war had imposed, but with talks going on and a ceasefire in place, people began to relax.

All [our] vehicles are running except the Datsun '73 whose parts I am trying to fix up to bring it back on the road. The vehicles still ply the Fadugu–Makeni route. Income from their activities is low. We have also started buying goods from Freetown and sell to some of the places we used to operate before the war intensified. Profit has been very, very low over the years and was used to maintain the family.

Well, thanks to God for all these because we are still well and living. Others are dead now or part of their body mutilated. We are really struggling to be in business. It is hard.

I had really welcomed the news when you said maybe we could try a spare parts business in the future. But with the high custom duty rate I don't see a possibility in the nearest future. I could remember when [we got] Datsun '73 in 1991, our effort to get a duty-free concession was frustrated. And today this is the only arm of the government that could earn money especially when the mining and produce sectors have been adversely affected since the war started. The security position remains unpredictable. Foday Sankoh and his R.U.F. rebels continue to violate [the] cease-fire agreement.

With all these above factors I don't see an atmosphere of peace in [the] near future not to say any development that can improve the life of Sierra Leoneans. That is why I have said time and again that staying here is a waste of time. I want to make use of this time to go abroad and do something better so that by the time I could return things would have taken their proper shape. Sometime in my quiet moments I cry for my country. I really want to leave.

Umaru Mansaray
Freetown, June 12, 1996

Paramount Chief Alimamy Fana II

Chapter Eight
PLUNDER OF THE INNOCENTS

S ierra Leone's new president set off on a rocky road. The army, ambivalent at best about ceding power, would still cast an ominous shadow. The country's culture of corruption would have to be reformed or democracy would succumb to privilege. Talks with the rebels needed the touch of a sage if the war were to be concluded. And even if the miracle of peace were to come, repairing the destruction of five years of fighting, the ruined economy and shattered lives, would exhaust a billionaire's portfolio and the patience of a saint.

The sixty-four-year-old president was a Mandingo from Kailahun District, currently the headquarters of the Revolutionary United Front. His ethnicity had helped to make the Sierra Leone People's Party more palatable to voters in the north who generally viewed the SLPP as a strictly Mende affair. It didn't hurt that he was Alhaji Kabbah, the first Muslim head of state in a country where Islam had steadily strengthened its numbers.

In his youth Kabbah had attended school in Freetown before heading off to Wales to earn a degree in economics. Back in Sierra Leone he joined the colonial administration in 1959 and remained in the civil service after independence. He eventually returned to the United Kingdom to earn a law degree and then, in 1971, joined the United Nations Development Programme where he worked for the next twenty years. A slender, reserved man, he appeared to lack the gregarious disposition usually required of a politician. Instead, he brought the steady hand of a bureaucrat to the president's office, and more importantly, a reputation for being honest.

President Kabbah moved quickly to keep the peace talks on track. At his April 1996 meeting with Foday Sankoh, he and the RUF leader had established a framework to guide their respective negotiators. By June, a member of the government team reported that the two sides had worked out twenty-six of twenty-eight provisions of a peace accord.

While the talks adjourned for the parties to reconsider the sticking points—the most critical being the presence of foreign troops aiding the government—Sierra Leone's recalcitrant army began to bridle. Soon after taking office Kabbah had replaced commanders installed by the former NPRC regime with more seasoned, higher ranking officers. Then in September some in the lower ranks tried to stage a coup in apparent retaliation. Six soldiers were arrested and some 140 forced to retire. The coup plot heightened mistrust of the military within the fledgling Kabbah administration. Soldiers from Nigeria began to guard the president. Civil defense forces, the Kamajo hunters in particular, appeared to supplant the regular army as the country's primary defender.

THE KAMAJO, a male-only society of the Mende people, traditionally hunted bush game—monkeys, deer, fowl—with an assortment of knives and ancient shotguns and rifles. Their emergence as a fighting force dated from around 1993 when an activist from Kenema, Dr. Alpha Lavalie, began to organize the hunters to defend civilians from rebel attacks. The thought that people rooted in their communities, with intimate knowledge of local terrain, would provide protection superior to that of the army proved to be true. Lavalie was soon assassinated for his efforts, but the civil defense movement continued to grow.

In the Southern Province chiefdom of Jaiama Bongor, one Samuel Hinga Norman, a retired army captain and current regent chief, deployed local Kamajo to keep the rebels away. Back in 1967 Norman was a young lieutenant who, as aide-de-camp to Governor-General Henry Lightfoot Boston, had obeyed his force commander's order to place the new prime minister, Siaka Stevens, under house arrest—the start of Sierra Leone's first coup d'etat. With the swearing-in of Tejan Kabbah as president, Norman was appointed deputy minister of defense with a mandate to expand the civil defense forces.

Norman was superbly effective. According to some estimates, the Kamajos and other civil defense forces soon outnumbered the army. An explosive rivalry quickly developed leading to occasional outbreaks of fighting between the supposed allies. More importantly, the Kamajo began to attack the rebels. During September and October, despite the agreement to cease fire while peace talks proceeded, Kamajo units, assisted by Executive Outcomes, overran several RUF bases in the south and east, including Foday Sankoh's headquarters known as The Zogoda.

With their fighters retreating in disarray, Sankoh and his negotiators rapidly concluded the peace agreement with the government. It remained to be seen if the deal was genuine or simply an RUF tactic for buying time, but in Abidjan on November 30, 1996, Kabbah and Sankoh signed an accord that purported to end the war.

> Though the peace accord between the R.U.F. and our government had been signed, [a] series of cease fire violations have taken [place] causing loss of life and property. My [ancestral] village is one of those suffering from this cease fire violation. The rebels have refused to hand in their weapons to our soldiers. They say they will only hand in their weapons to a U.N. monitoring team. The big question now that everyone is asking, when will this U.N. monitoring team be deployed? When will our civilian government provide logistics to the rebels that will make them hand in their weapons?
>
> There are a lot of security problems in the country, such as armed robbery, house breaking and larceny, ambushes, abductions, kidnapping, etc. However, the situation is much better than it was before.... Though life in Sierra Leone is difficult, especially after the war, my wife and myself are struggling hard to maintain the family.
>
> A.K. Bangura
Fadugu, Feb. 24, 1997

• • •

THE PEACE ACCORD called for the rebels to report to designated camps where they were to turn in their weapons and begin the process of integration into the broader society. They would be allocated seats on a new Commission for the Consolidation of Peace and a reorganized National Electoral Commission but no representation in parliament or the administration. The RUF would have to remake itself into a political party and select candidates to contest for elective office just like the established parties.

For the government's part, it would ask Executive Outcomes and other foreign forces to leave Sierra Leone. In addition, Sankoh and his rebels would be granted immunity from prosecution for their crimes. Selected soldiers from the RUF and the armed forces of Sierra Leone would be combined to form a brand new national army.

If the agreement had been hard to hammer out, its implementation would prove still harder. The international community, principally the United Nations and the Organization of African Unity, had been helpful mediators in Abidjan, but they committed little money and less manpower to insure that the parties kept their word. A team of outside observers—the Neutral Monitoring Group—called for in the peace agreement was never established. RUF fighters were extremely reluctant to surrender their weapons to government soldiers. Furthermore, the accord failed to even mention the potent Kamajo hunters. For his part, President Kabbah asked Executive Outcomes to leave shortly after the accord was signed. This alleviated one of Foday Sankoh's primary concerns but left Kabbah's own regime dangerously vulnerable.

Something of a standoff developed in the early months of 1997. It wasn't exactly peace, but there was also little war. Hundreds of hopeful refugees began to make their way home from Guinea and Liberia. Many more, displaced within Sierra Leone itself, set out to reclaim what was left of abandoned homes or to look for lost loved ones.

> I am glad that you were able to see [on television] some of the
> destruction in our country during the five years of war. What

you saw in that programme may just be about 1/10th of what actually happened.

Last week, a friend of mine who is a military officer forced me to go home and see the extent of the rebel destruction in my [ancestral] village. Both of us left Fadugu on the 18 March '97, and when we reached home, it took me some time to know where my father's house was, and my house too. I had to cry literally. The entire village was completely destroyed. Almost all the houses were burnt down to ashes. Nobody has gone to settle there yet, because the rebels of the R.U.F. are still around that area.

The war affected every part of Sierra Leone, but the worst affected areas are the East, South, and Tonkolili District in the North. Government is talking of resettlement and rehabilitation, but it will take a long time before it could be completed. For now and in the years to come, government is concentrating in the East and South, and then to the North.

For now Fadugu is my home village, because there is not a single chair, bed, house, etc. left in my village. Worst of it all, not a single sheet of corrugated iron [for roofing] was left both in my father's house and mine. My relatives and myself have decided to build temporary shelters while starting life afresh. There is nothing wrong in my garden, and so I am determined to continue with [that] work late this year.

> A.K. Bangura
> Fadugu, March 24, 1997

Like the peace agreement it had just concluded, the government of Tejan Kabbah appeared to lack sufficient underpinning. Its security apparatus broke up two new coup plots during the month of January. Soon afterward the government reduced the allocation of rice for the army and police. Whether or not it was meant to be, most soldiers viewed the cut as retaliation.

On the other side, the RUF had its own problems with insubordination. On March 2, Foday Sankoh arrived unexpectedly at the airport in Lagos, Nigeria. Why he had gone there unannounced, since Nigeria had allied itself with the Sierra Leone government, remains a matter of speculation. Sankoh later claimed he had gone to solicit support for the peace agreement, but that was news to the Nigerians. Surprised officials hustled Sankoh off to the capital, Abuja, and placed him under house arrest. Two weeks later, a faction of the RUF announced that Sankoh had been ousted from the movement's leadership. His would-be replacement, Philip Palmer, and two RUF members of the new peace commission loyal to Palmer then trekked to a rebel base in Kailahun District where they were warmly greeted and promptly imprisoned.

Confusion prevailed for more than a month as the leaderless RUF and the precarious government of Sierra Leone each labored to achieve equilibrium. Then, on Sunday morning May 25, Freetown residents awoke to the sound of gunfire. Mutinous government soldiers had laid siege to the prison at Pademba Road in the central city. They quickly overpowered a small contingent of guards and freed all the inmates. Conspicuous among the liberated were several soldiers who had been accused in the previous September's coup plot. The mutineers moved on to State House where they drove off the government's Nigerian protectors in a hail of bullets. President Kabbah fled across the border to Guinea, while the soldiers and many of Freetown's civilians joined in an orgy of plunder.

A sad and battered Freetown emerged from the smoke of battle. Bullet-riddled bodies lay in the streets, especially around State House. Looters had ransacked many retail shops and killed at least two of their Lebanese owners. Wealthy residents had been relieved of their cars and most of their household possessions. Hungry and greedy alike had emptied warehouses stocked for the feeding of refugees. In addition, the upper floors of the Bank of Sierra Leone and the entire treasury building had been destroyed in what looked suspiciously like an effort to thwart a current investigation of corruption.

Although they were roundly condemned both at home and abroad, the soldiers announced that they had set up an Armed Forces Revolutionary Council (AFRC) to run the country. It would be led by one of those freed from Pademba Road, Major Johnny Paul Koroma.

The new AFRC suspended parliament, banned the Kamajo militias, and invited the RUF rebels to join them. From his place of confinement in Nigeria, Foday Sankoh endorsed the coup. RUF fighters began to drift into Freetown to grab their own share of the loot and take up positions alongside government soldiers.

Accustomed as they were to cowing the people, the soldiers failed to reckon with their anger. Sierra Leoneans generally loathed the army as corrupt, incapable of winning the war and unlikely to deliver good government. The junta's invitation to the RUF merely confirmed what many suspected: the soldiers were collaborating with the enemy. Freetown's shops remained shuttered, its markets empty, schools and offices closed.

Within hours of the coup, President Kabbah, then in the Guinean capital of Conakry, appealed to Nigeria for help. This would put Nigeria, led by the despot Sani Abacha who himself had come to power in a coup d'etat, in the peculiar position of attempting to restore democracy in Sierra Leone. Nigeria responded on June 2 with a jet bomber attack on AFRC headquarters at Cockerill Barracks in Freetown's west end, and either poorly aimed or wantonly indiscriminate shelling of the east end by gunboats in the Sierra Leone River. Civilians, not the army, bore the brunt of these attacks.

The same day in apparent retaliation, AFRC/RUF soldiers routed a company of Nigerians from the Mammy Yoko Hotel near Lumley Beach where they had established a base from which to remove foreigners to a nearby US warship. While several hundred potential evacuees huddled in the hotel basement, the combined force of army and rebels launched a fierce assault that pulverized much of the building above. Following this embarrassment Nigeria began to transfer additional troops to Sierra Leone, most of them from its ECOMOG peacekeeping contingent in Liberia where the war had ended and one-time rebel leader Charles Taylor was about to be elected president.

The Kabbah government set up a radio station at Lungi Airport, still under Nigerian control, to rally the people to resist. Most civilians withheld cooperation from the junta, and foreign governments refused to recognize it. At the end of August, the Economic Community of West African States imposed a trade embargo on Sierra Leone to be enforced by a blockade. In October the UN Security Council voted its own prohibition on shipments of arms and oil and banned travel by AFRC members.

With reinforcements in place at their Lungi encampment and at Jui a few miles east of Freetown, Nigerian troops, now officially under the ECOMOG banner, zealously enforced the embargoes. Low-flying jets strafed ships that dared to run the blockade. On at least one occasion the port itself came under attack. Clashes with junta soldiers erupted around Freetown's outskirts. Refugees streamed into the countryside only to meet fighting between junta forces and the Kamajo.

The embargoes swiftly choked the city. Two principal commodities, rice and petroleum, evaporated as did the supply of money to buy them. Hunger spread across Freetown even as the soldiers satiated themselves by robbing civilians.

Gradually, the embargoes and general strike forced the junta's hand. Starved for funds and popular support, the leaders decided to negotiate. Talks in Conakry between representatives of the junta and ECOWAS, without Kabbah's participation, produced a settlement at the end of October. The soldiers agreed to the reinstatement of Kabbah's government in seven months; fighting was to cease immediately; all combatants would disarm by the end of December; junta troops would be granted immunity from prosecution; and Foday Sankoh was "expected to return to his country to make his contribution to the peace process."

> It's a long time now since I last wrote you due to the military take-over in Sierra Leone, and the subsequent sanctions that followed.
>
> It may surprise you to hear that most Sierra Leoneans were expecting either a civil war or a military take-over, because the civilian government of Tejan Kabbah totally lost confidence in the army and so there was no good relationship between the national army and the government. Because of this, the

government started to raise its own army [the Kamajo], but it was tribalistically based and so most ethnic groups were not happy about it. There were conflicts here and there, and this made the government most unpopular.

I know you people over there are wondering how we are living, how our positions are in terms of work, health and security. It is indeed a terrible and most deplorable situation.

Since May 25 this year, everything is at a standstill. No schooling, no serious government work, no payment of workers' salary. I stopped receiving salary in March, that was before the military junta and it was only last week that I was given a month's salary. There is a complete shortage of all food items in Sierra Leone. A gallon of petrol is now sold at Le10,000.00 [about $13] while that of kerosene is going at Le6,000 [nearly $8], and by next week it will be between Le20,000.00 and Le16,000.00 respectively. Most of us no longer rely on government work. I work assiduously to maintain my home. I make small rice farm, grow cassava, yam and maize. My twin boys are very hard working, they do most of the work as I am getting older.

When the civilian government of Alhaji Tejan Kabbah is restored in April next year, we expect assistance from friends like you to help us educate our children.

> A.K. Bangura
> Fadugu, Nov. 14, 1997

No salaries for teachers or civil servants, no commodities in the marketplace, and no money in people's pockets meant no business for Bangura's neighbors the Mansaray brothers. They began selling off possessions, including two of their three trucks, to the few who could still afford them.

Events in S.L. to say the least is not encouraging. The military and the R.U.F. rebels have turned against the people of this country. They have continued to kill, maim, burn houses, loot, rape, harass and even destroy the country. It is the most difficult time in our history. We are now running [out] of food, medicine, fuel and other important commodities. We pray to the Lord to stop our suffering now.

Before May 25, 1997, I [have been] working through your help to leave this country. That hope was destroyed when the military took over our democratically elected Gov't. Now that this thing (peace) is not forthcoming, I still want you to try other means [for me] to leave S.L. for the U.S.A.

The obstacles to peace in S.L. are many and [peace is] not easy to obtain. This because the present leaders are not committed to peace. They are other groups of murderers, thieves and bandits. We will never trust these people.

There is no business now, everything has been destroyed. The economy is zero or below. I want to appeal to you again to please consider my exodus.

Umaru Mansaray
Fadugu, Nov. 12, 1997

As the situation grew more desperate, other Fadugu people, some of whom hadn't been steady correspondents, began to write.

I am sorry for not writing to you for quite awhile now. However, I promise to write often though there isn't at the moment any proper mail system operating in our country due to the present political impasse.

I always think of you and our old good days together while you were in Sierra Leone. I enjoyed your company and I fully appreciated your kindness and friendship....

My children are now in form three—junior secondary school 3—[and were supposed] to take the basic education certificate examination in June/July this year, but the whole educational system was interrupted by the May 25 military takeover. There is no proper schooling here at the moment for both primary and secondary schools and even colleges and universities still remain closed....

I am kindly asking you for a green card lottery [form] to live and work in the U.S.A. which is offered in the new U.S.

government lottery. Please send a post card to your national visa service. May God help.

Y.S. Mansaray
Fadugu, Nov. 22, 1997

With this entreaty Y.S. Mansaray, the grandson of Fadugu's founder, joined thousands of others in the search for a way out.

FREETOWN'S FOREIGN EMBASSIES had always experienced brisk visa traffic, but in the war years the crowds outside their gates ballooned. At the United States embassy, down the hill from State House in the Cotton Tree's embrace, people gathered early for the long and nearly always futile wait. The US had long been subject to the myth of easy living, concocted mainly by Hollywood producers and Sierra Leonean immigrants. Big screen fantasies and pictures of stateside brothers and sisters in fine clothes and fancy cars fostered false perceptions among those still at home. But the nation of immigrants was stingy with its visas, especially in poor countries like Sierra Leone.

Most who queued for hours, or sometimes days, to apply for visitor or student visas would ultimately be rejected on the grounds that the interviewing officer felt the applicant would never return to Sierra Leone. After that, the annual "green card" or diversity visa lottery, instituted by the US Congress in 1994 to allocate 55,000 permanent visas for the world's masses, provided the only other chance to escape to America. On the yearly ration of some 21,000 visas for the entire continent of Africa, Y.S. Mansaray and thousands of war-weary others would place their hope.

During the coup's disorderly aftermath, Freetown's embassies ceased to be beacons. With their gates padlocked and personnel evacuated, they languished alongside the city's idle offices and shops. A few lucky families paid exorbitant fees to board ships bound for Conakry, or Banjul farther north in Gambia. Others walked for days to reach the Guinea border. Everyone else had to wait out the siege.

◆ ◆ ◆

THE NEW YEAR 1998 began with little optimism. The AFRC/RUF junta, despite its pronouncements to the contrary, seemed reluctant to relinquish the capital. Strapped for cash, the soldiers "paid themselves" by robbing the people of what little they had left. In one notorious episode, several officers burglarized the embassy of Iran. Junta leaders apologized to Iran and disciplined the perpetrators, but ordinary citizens received no such courtesy.

Tension heightened at the end of January when junta soldiers clashed with the Kamajo near Bo and Kenema. Rumors swirled about Freetown. A force of exiles was said to be organizing in Conakry and would soon attack.* The jittery junta threatened to stay in power unless Foday Sankoh was allowed to come to Freetown and Nigeria reduced the number of ECOMOG soldiers it had amassed outside the city.

On Thursday, February 5, fighting erupted near the town of Hastings, about six miles east of the capital. Conflicting claims obscure the cause, but ECOMOG forces pushed, and when the junta's line gave, ECOMOG pushed some more. Throughout the weekend, ECOMOG soldiers crept along the main road toward Freetown's eastern edge and fanned out into the rugged hills that overlook the city. By the following Tuesday, a full-scale battle for the high ground raged near the village of Leicester. Mortar and rocket fire echoed from the hills as ECOMOG jets swooped above.

Shelling grew heavier as the week wore on, raining fire on the city itself. Civilians seemed expendable as the two armies emptied their arsenals. Terrified residents huddled in their homes, praying for protection from the blitz. ECOMOG forces took Cline Town in the east end, and moved on the city center. Thursday the twelfth, the junta aban-

---

* This particular rumor proved to be true. It was later revealed that the UK Foreign Office had arranged to ship arms to forces loyal to Kabbah through the private firm Sandline International, which was closely tied to Branch Energy and Executive Outcomes. The deal caused a scandal in Britain because the arrangement, albeit in support of Sierra Leone's elected government, violated the international embargo on arms shipments to the region.

doned State House, its soldiers scattering into the hills and down the peninsula. By the weekend, ten days after it had started, the battle of Freetown was over.

The torrent of bullets and artillery shells left the city badly scarred. Many of its old clapboard houses had burned, and what was left of shops and supermarkets was looted once again. Civilian casualties looked surprisingly light, however; by one estimate around 100 had died and perhaps 1000 wounded. Hungry, weary residents poured into the streets to celebrate their liberation.

President Kabbah returned to Freetown on March 10, following a brief transition led by Vice-President Albert Joe Demby. With his benefactor, Sani Abacha, and various other dignitaries at his side, Kabbah pledged to "make this a new beginning for Sierra Leone."

The task would be nearly insurmountable. Freetown was free again, but angry bands of soldier-rebels marauded in the countryside. A week after they fled the capital, the sobels attacked Bo. Combined elements of ECOMOG and the Kamajo secured the town only after several days of fierce fighting. In central Sierra Leone, the important town of Bumbuna, home of the country's unfinished hydroelectric project, and several nearby villages were raided at the end of February. In April the sobels vented their wrath on diamond-rich Kono District. Médecins Sans Frontières and the Red Cross reported a surge of refugees suffering severed ears and limbs.

FADUGU DURING THE WAR functioned like a tidal basin, absorbing the swell of kinsfolk dislodged by fighting to the south then returning them to their homes during times of relative calm. Now, with the sobels amuck in the countryside, the inward flow grew heavy. The war was drawing closer. Returnees talked about the sobels' vow of revenge: "operation no living thing."

Joy at the junta's ouster quickly transformed to fear. Mammy Thor closed her kiosk and went to stay with relatives at a house she owned in Makeni, where a large ECOMOG force seemed to offer more security.

Mindful of the rebels' predilection for kidnapping children and raping girls and women, Umaru Mansaray moved his wife, Mabinty, to Makeni along with three-year-old Mohamed, and the family's newest addition, a boy named Lamini. Umaru's brother Alie sent his oldest son with them. Umaru and Alie stayed in Fadugu for the moment to conduct what business they could.

In the middle of May, the Mansaray brothers decided to gamble. They needed goods in order to sell, and Freetown was the place to get them. Umaru boarded one of the few lorries still making the dreaded journey, where a tree in the roadway or the thunder of the vehicle's wheels on a hidden sheet of metal almost certainly foreshadowed an ambush.

Safe in the battle-scarred capital he began his search for supplies. Many shops remained closed, victims of looting or abandoned by their owners, but others had begun to do business again, although prices reflected scarcity. Merchants restocked using chartered boats to fetch goods from up the coast at Conakry. Demand was so strong that some items never made it into shops, selling directly at the wharf instead. Umaru bought the staples: rice, sugar, salt, margarine, condensed milk, batteries, matches, Vaseline for dry skin, and sweets for the palate. Having left his own truck in the safety of Fadugu, he hired one in Freetown to take the goods home.

The well-laded truck departed late Thursday, May 21, arriving in Fadugu around 3:00 AM. Family members pitched in to unload the heavy cargo then promptly went to bed. A short while later, gunfire disrupted their slumber. The sound seemed distant at first, still Umaru and Alie's mother joined the steady stream of people making for the village of Sangbanba two miles to the south.

The brothers stayed for the moment. Should they move their truck for safety? They weren't sure what to do. Shots were getting closer now. The Nigerian soldiers stationed in the town appeared to be inching backward from positions to the north and east. Umaru sent his driver to get the truck from down Kasasi Road at the north edge of town. Its engine roared to life only to die in a hundred yards. Armed men stepped into the road motioning the driver out. He leaped from the cab and ran for his life.

Everyone was running now. Bullets whizzed through the center of town. Flat on his belly, Umaru slithered out the back door of his house. He scrambled across the yard and down a steep slope into the family rice swamp. Now out of the line of fire, he got up and ran. At One Mile, Fadugu's western outskirts, he joined the panicked, southward sprint. Over his shoulder plumes of black smoke painted a somber sky.

> It is a long time since I wrote you a letter. It was mainly due to the 9-month Junta rule which brought this nation to standstill and caused the worst human tragedy ever on the people of Sierra Leone.
>
> After they were kicked out of power by ECOMOG in Freetown they continued with their atrocities up-country. They killed, maimed, raped, looted, and destroyed property of people. This is the most senseless war I have ever heard of. Presently they still continue with their mayhem by chopping off the hands, ears, noses, and limbs of people.
>
> It was this same Junta/RUF that entered Fadugu on May 22, this year at 6:30 A.M. I was woken up that morning by sporadic gun fire. When I came out everybody was running here and there. I had nothing to do but to flee for my life. As I fled, all our three houses were looted and burnt down to ashes. It was painful to see all what we had worked for all these years has gone in vain.
>
> Umaru Mansaray
> Freetown, June 12, 1998

Y.S. Mansaray

Chapter Nine
CARNAGE IN THE STREETS

Perhaps the rebels would have raided Fadugu anyway, but the veneer of security the Nigerians provided ultimately provoked the attack. The aggressive Nigerian soldiers had scoured the bush for rebels. Lucky suspects would be harassed or detained, but many others were simply killed. During the war years, caprice came to override the values of civil society.

As he ran to the northwest, Fadugu's chief, Alimamy Fana II, must have seen the bitter clouds billowing above the town. To his credit, Chief Fana had stayed with his people instead of retreating to Freetown. Now he and many more made their way along the road toward the ancient village of Kasasi. From there they could continue all the way to Guinea if necessary.

This time they wouldn't go that far. After a few miles the chief and those with him decided to sit and wait. A Nigerian-manned Alpha Jet, a small subsonic fighter bomber, screamed overhead. Called in by the retreating ground troops, the jet dived toward Fadugu, spewing fire at anything that moved. But by then the rebels had gone. The jet merely added its own measure of destruction.

When the shooting subsided and the smoke had drifted away, the chief and the others cautiously made their way back along Kasasi Road. In Fadugu they found several survivors, including Y.S. Mansaray who had hidden with his brother in a grove of palms only yards from the attackers.

> You might have heard over the BBC or VOA about the
> RUF/AFRC Junta attacks on Fadugu town. The first attack

was launched on May 22, leaving 27 dead, burning 82 houses and abducting several boys and girls. Our two houses along the Makeni–Kabala highway were completely burnt down including personal belongings and household items and cooking utensils. The teachers' residences and one of the [medical] treatment centre buildings were burnt. My uncle and one of my colleague teachers, Mr. Alpha D. Kalokoh, and his younger brother were brutally murdered in that attack.

Y.S. Mansaray
Fadugu, Oct. 19, 1998

From Sangbanba to the south, Umaru Mansaray had hiked along the main road toward Makeni. He saw A.K. Bangura, shaken but alive, near the village of Kanikay, some eleven miles from Fadugu. Then he caught a lift on a motorbike down to Makeni where he gave the sad news to his family.

One week later, Umaru reluctantly returned to Fadugu. He found his brother Alie alive, but their truck and three houses had all been burned and the new goods for their business, stolen by the rebels. Alie hid in the bush during the day of the attack then came back to the village at night to sleep amid the ruins. His wife and youngest son fled all the way to Makeni.

When the rebels torched a house, what actually caught fire were furnishings, clothes, wooden shutters (window glass was an extremely rare luxury) and doors, and the rafters holding the roof. Heat from the blaze and disintegration of the rafters buckled the corrugated sheets of metal roofing and brought them crashing down in a heap. Then tropical rains went to work on mud walls, eroding them back to the earth. The fortunate few with cement block walls would at least have a shell to re-cover. Most, if they couldn't hurry to beat the rains, would need to begin from scratch, forming moistened soil into blocks to make new walls and cutting trees in the bush for new rafters.

"We have repaired one house out of the three burnt houses," Umaru reported in his letter describing the attack.

> We had to use the old zinc and nails [and] sticks from the bush. Some members of the family have already gone back. But my wife and children and Alie's children will stay in Freetown.

Umaru's otherwise grim letter also contained some heartening news.

> I was lucky to win the U.S.A. DV-99 immigrant lottery. The processing of the documents will start on October 1, 1998– Sept. 30, 1999. By next week I will photocopy some of the documents and send them to you for you to look at.

> Umaru Mansaray
> Freetown, June 12, 1998

At last Umaru had found a way out. If he completed the complex paperwork without flaw, survived the required interview, and came up with the necessary cash for fees and transportation, he and his family would move to the United States sometime in the next year. That is, if the war didn't intervene. Now they would have to stay in the capital to keep in touch with the process.

FREETOWN OFFERED precious little comfort for newcomers from up-country. Jammed with refugees and battered by the fighting that restored the civilian government, the crumbling city lacked in every way. Banks had reopened, critical supplies had begun to trickle in, and some repairs were being made, but conditions were still the worst since the city's early days as a haven for freed slaves. Adding to the uneasiness was the government's decision to prosecute captured junta soldiers and their alleged collaborators.

A series of treason trials kicked off in April, with the appearance in court of eighteen accused collaborators: three employees of the Sierra Leone Broadcasting Service, who stayed on the job during the junta's sojourn; former BBC broadcaster Hilton Fyle, who operated a private radio station in Freetown; I.B. Kargbo, the proprietor of the independent *New Citizen* newspaper; and assorted business people, lawyers, and civilian members of the junta government. More than one observer pointed out that President Kabbah, who himself had worked for the previous military government which also came to power in a coup, now wished to try, perhaps even execute, others who had made a similar choice.

With that in mind, the current situation seemed to demand a certain degree of prudence. The journalists, in particular, had appeared to simply be doing their jobs by giving voice to opinions on all sides. Nevertheless, after eight years of war and nine months of the hated junta, Sierra Leoneans had little patience for discussions about constitutional rights and an unfettered press. The trial proceeded with broad public support.

At the beginning of September the verdicts came down: sixteen guilty and two acquittals. All the guilty were sentenced to die. Another batch of defendants that included former president Momoh—he had returned home the previous year and was accused of advising the junta—was convicted at a second trial. Momoh received a ten-year prison term while another sixteen were handed death sentences.

These civilians would at least be granted the formality of an appeal. Twenty-four members of the army sentenced to death by a court-martial weren't so lucky. In mid-October the condemned soldiers, including one woman and a brother of AFRC leader Johnny Paul Koroma, were hauled down the peninsula near the ocean-side village of Goderich where, before a jeering crowd, they were tied to posts and shot.

The spate of death sentences and hasty executions undermined the international sympathy Kabbah had so diligently cultivated. Amnesty International denounced the executions while Britain and a number of other countries expressed concern. Most Sierra Leoneans, on the other hand, supported the government's action. The people who had suffered so much were in no mood for clemency.

Through it all, the president appeared to be unusually withdrawn. His wife of some thirty years, Patricia Kabbah, had died in early May. A formidable personage in her own right—a lawyer, fluent in French, with a master's degree besides—she was the president's closest confidante and advisor. Whether her death accounted for the president's behavior is a matter of speculation, but afterward he was seldom seen in public. He spoke on the radio a few times, but for several months he seemed to prefer the seclusion of his home at the expense of restoring his regime.

In the midst of the group trials Sierra Leone's most notorious transgressor also came to court. Nigeria released Foday Sankoh to the custody of the Kabbah government, and he appeared before a Freetown judge in the middle of September. Following a brief trial on an eight-count charge of treason, Sankoh too was found guilty and sentenced to death. Meanwhile, his rebels upped the tenor of their attacks.

AT KABALA IN AUGUST, a team of ECOMOG soldiers prepared to accept the surrender of a number of rebels who had apparently grown tired of the struggle. When the appointed hour arrived, the rebels approached the ECOMOG position under a white flag to turn in their weapons. Suddenly the flag hit the ground, and the rebels opened fire. Soon after this deadly deception, the rebels revisited Fadugu.

> The second attack was launched on Sept. 11 [1998]. 61 houses were burnt, 6 persons killed including our paramount chief, Alimamy Fana II, who was burnt alive in his residence (1:35 AM).
>
> My residence was also burnt down, including all my personal belongings (clothes, beds, mattress, boxes, to name a few) and all other personal belongings of my wife and children. We are at the moment staying with one of my relatives in Fadugu.
>
> There is yet no schooling going on in the entire Koinadugu District. These attacks have made life very difficult for the entire inhabitants in the region. Everything economically, socially, and culturally has been disrupted also.
>
> I am at the moment very much stranded. My children need to continue schooling elsewhere relatively safe or calm. I need extra help or assistance elsewhere. There is no aid or grant from the government at the moment.
>
> Y.S. Mansaray
Fadugu, October 19, 1998

Chief Fana had refused to run again. He would die with his people if it came to that. And so in September it had. His grisly murder, the absence of other village elders—most of who had decamped for safer ground—and the massive destruction of property dashed all hope for the moment. "Fadugu is no more," Umaru Mansaray had sobbed into the telephone following the first attack. Now that seemed to be true. Few would venture back to re-occupy the place, at least until peace was assured. But as 1998 drew to a close, peace was only a dream.

YEARS BEFORE, when the Mansaray brothers' business was taking off, Umaru had begun to rent a room on Kissy Road, a street of tottering wood houses mixed with muscular cement block structures in Freetown's crowded east end. The room would insure him lodging during his frequent buying trips to the city. Now, he and his family settled into it temporarily before moving, a couple of weeks later, to less cramped quarters a few houses down the street.

Their application to emigrate to the United States proceeded with only a minor glitch. Umaru originally registered his wife as Mabinty Fofana, since Mabinty, like many married women in Sierra Leone, had retained her birth name. The couple, knowing the American custom of the wife taking her husband's last name, decided that Mabinty should be a Mansaray too. Following an exchange of letters, US immigration authorities agreed that this was permissible. As the new year dawned, the year of their liberation, all they had to do was wait to be scheduled for an interview.

Freetown remained tense in early January as reports of RUF attacks up-country flowed in with each wave of refugees. The fearful city recoiled under a curfew from 10:00 in the evening until 7:00 the following morning. Streets that once pulsed with a vibrant night life now idled in eerie silence.

Around 3:00 in the morning of Wednesday, January 6, Umaru awoke to an unusual clatter. From his second-floor perch he could see a stream of crowded vehicles and bundle-laden pedestrians rushing westward toward the center of town. The numbers only increased as the sky began to brighten. By 5:00 AM gunshots could be heard in the distance. An hour later they exploded outside the door. Umaru could see the "ragtag gun toters" now. "You said we are not going to enter the city," he remembered hearing them yell, "but we are here again. We are in control. You are under us."

Sometime later, perhaps around half-past seven, rebel soldiers began pounding on doors and gates. "Everyone come out," they called. "If you don't come out we will kill you." Fear collided with the need for self-control as Umaru and Mabinty descended the stairs. Were they about to have their sons snatched away by the pernicious RUF? Or watch the women led off to be violated by a rabble of soldiers? Or feel the swing of a matchet as it scalded its way through an arm? Their dream of new life in America dissolved in a bloody blur.

"We are the RUF. We have come to take over," a rebel commander declared. They had come in peace, he told the disbelieving crowd. Everyone should support them. Then he asked for a moment of silence for a commander who had been killed earlier that morning. With that the rebels moved on.

The tension eased in an eddy of sighs. For the moment there would be no butchery on this street. Instead the rebels vented their wrath on Freetown's symbols of power. A couple of blocks from the Mansarays', they torched the Eastern Police Station. A building in the center of town that housed several government ministries went up in smoke soon after, followed by the Criminal Investigations Department on Pademba Road. Farther along Pademba Road rebels opened the prison gates. Jubilant inmates, including those recently condemned for collaborating with the AFRC junta, danced into the early morning sunshine.

Like many of his neighbors on that first malignant morning, Umaru ventured cautiously out to see for himself what was happening. All that he had heard was true. The rebels had even set fire to Big Market (the basket market) down near government wharf. How, he wondered, did they hope to govern if the infrastructure of society was destroyed? Even more puzzling was the absence of response from ECOMOG. What were their Nigerian protectors doing?

The RUF, it seems, had tricked the ECOMOG forces. They had attacked in the early morning at Calaba Town some three miles east of the capital. As local residents ran from the fighting, the rebels, dressed in civilian clothes, joined their flight through ECOMOG lines. The rebels abandoned larger weapons and concealed small arms in what looked like bundles of household possessions. To ECOMOG they were indistinguishable from refugees. Once in the city, they were said to have rearmed at an east end cemetery where they dug up rifle-filled coffins that had been buried like so many war dead.

"We wanted the people of Freetown to feel the heat of war," rebel commander Sam "Mosquito" Bockarie* told *West Africa* by satellite phone. "Once they've felt this heat they'll start thinking of peace." But peace would not come soon. From their western base at Wilberforce, ECOMOG began to counterattack.

The second day, Thursday, January 7, Freetown's streets were left to the fighters. Government radio at Lungi, where the president and most of his ministers had re-located, warned that anyone caught outside would be considered a rebel. Foday Sankoh was taken from his secret jail, thought to be somewhere in Guinea, to meet with Kabbah at Lungi. The two soon announced a ceasefire agreement, but it had no effect on the fighting. The rebels rampaged while ECOMOG flew in fresh troops from Nigeria and Ghana.

At Kissy Road the Mansarays, like most of Freetown's residents, simply waited to see what would happen. With rebels roaming the streets and ECOMOG vowing to drive them out, there was little to do but pray. The family had a bag of ground cassava, known as *gari*, but nothing else to eat. The two adults and Mohamed, now four years old, could endure the meager menu, but Lamini, the newest son who was not yet two, didn't understand why there was no rice. As his crying increased and the days of confinement dragged on, Mabinty risked six blocks of heart-pounding terror to scavenge a few cups of the precious grain at the nearly deserted Dove Cot Market.

---

* Bockarie was also known as "Maskita," the Krio rendering of "mosquito."

Day by day the rumble of battle drew nearer. ECOMOG advanced to reclaim the city one block, one neighborhood at a time. Each setback seemed to kindle the rebels' rage, and they punished civilians in return. Groups of rebels moved from house to crowded house, splashed them with gasoline, and dropped a match. Anyone who dared run from the inferno was shot. People caught on the street were brutally murdered, their bodies sometimes hacked to pieces.

As bullets began to fly around Kissy Road, fifteen or sixteen days into the siege, Umaru and Mabinty left their second-floor room to huddle with the families downstairs. There, a wall between the house and the street offered more protection. Soon afterward a grenade exploded in their abandoned upstairs room.

They could see the RUF outside. Rebel soldiers often sat near their gate during periods when the fighting diminished. Even as neighboring houses went up in flames and heads literally rolled in the streets, the rebels never entered their compound. The house was owned by a diamond dealer, and rumor had it that he moved stones for the rebels. "It was really a miracle for us to stay there up to the last minute unharmed," Umaru said.

Eighteen days after they entered the town, the rebels scattered in full retreat. ECOMOG soldiers appeared at the door asking for a drink of water. Umaru and Mabinty could come out now, they said. The danger had finally passed.

The city's destruction was almost impossible to comprehend. Hundreds of homes and buildings had been ruined. According to the *New York Times*, Connaught Hospital in the center of town had recorded 2,768 dead. There were likely hundreds more. Wheelbarrows plied the streets carting off corpses for burial. Many of the living had had hands cut off or suffered a vicious rape. Bodies and minds could never outlive these scars.

FREETOWN'S SENSE OF DREAD now shifted back to the countryside where the vanquished RUF was sure to take revenge. Scarcely a month later, a new correspondent from Fadugu, the son of an old teacher at the town's government primary school named A.B. Barrie, wrote in desperation.

> I am sorry to inform you that the rebels attacked us in the bushes and looted every bit of everything we have. We walked on foot from Fadugu to Guinea. [It] is about 100 and ten miles approximately. Severe hunger and starvation.... I am here with my wife and 3 children. Swollen foot and general body pain with the family and hunger....
>
> I and Dad departed from different directions running away from the rebels. So I am worried about him. So I am going to walk on foot again in search of him, for us to stay together. I heard that he is alive with severe suffering. I am leaving for Fadugu on the 10th of March, 1999, to walk on foot. I hope I will see him. His absence worries me a lot. I hope to return in Guinea on foot on the 15th April 1999, as my wife and children are all here suffering more from lack of food....
>
> The suffering is beyond what mind can picture. Please help us.
>
> Alie Barrie,
> Guinea, Feb. 2, 1999

It was unclear from his letter which attack had caused Barrie to flee, but reading his words there was no mistaking his pain. Others from Fadugu escaped to Guinea too, joining some 300,000 other Sierra Leoneans squeezed into villages and refugee camps along the border. The RUF had begun to regroup. Having failed to hold the capital, they would settle for lesser prey.

> Please be informed that I arrived in Freetown on June 29 from Conakry in the Republic of Guinea.
>
> The junta/rebels attacked Fadugu township for a third time on March 9 this year, leaving several people dead, destroying and burning houses (about 62 houses) and abducting men, women, and children. The house in which I was staying was burnt, including my personal belongings.
>
> The attack was launched in the early morning hours (at about 6:15 A.M.) by surprise while most of the people were still

sleeping in their houses. I narrowly escaped when my house was attacked. It was a serious attack. About 150 well-armed rebels were reported [to have] attacked the township. Two men were cruelly murdered on the spot. The one had his intestines/guts removed while the other had his head cut off and were left lying on the Makeni–Kabala motor highway. It was a very horrible scene. Some had their hands cut off and their bodies mutilated. In view of this dreadful event, I felt I was no longer safe to stay and moreover there was no house for me to reside [in].

Finally on March 13, I left Fadugu together with my friend Musa, his wife and children for the Republic of Guinea. We travelled on foot through various bush paths until we succeeded in arriving at a town called Sidakotor [Sittakotto] in Guinea where there was a large presence of the Guinean military forces. We were given free passage until we reached Conakry, the capital city, on April 19....

With the money you sent [in November] I was able to pay for my wife and children to travel to Freetown before the January 6 invasion by the rebels on Freetown. The balance amount of money was used for paying their tuition fees and other school charges. All of my children (Saidu, Umaru and Mariama) are attending the same school—Government Technical Institute at Congo Cross/Freetown which is not far away from the national stadium. Fatmata is in class four (IV) while the youngest one, Hawa, will be attending her first year by September. I must confess that all of them are doing well at school. And most important also was that all of them including their mother survived the January 6 invasion. The unfortunate event encountered was that their house [was] raided and properties looted by the rebels and their allies. However, I must be very grateful to God for protecting their lives throughout the period of the invasion. I am happy to be with them once again after separating for a period of about eight months.

Y.S. Mansaray
Freetown, July 6, 1999

• • •

APART FROM TERRORIZING the citizenry, the rebels' razing of
Freetown finally attracted international attention. The vague expres-
sions that a mention of Sierra Leone once evoked changed noticeably in
the dark days of January. Television brought the war into most Western
homes for the first time in its eight-year run. Growing public awareness
seemed to move political leaders to take a more active role in halting
the carnage. Britain, the United States, the United Nations, and the
Organization of African Unity all began to press for a settlement.

"The time has come to abandon hopes of a military victory and seek
a negotiated solution," the British foreign secretary, Robin Cook, was
reported to have told President Kabbah in March. Washington hosted
an RUF representative named Omrie Golley at the State Department
and initiated contact between him and Kabbah. The US also sent a special envoy, Jesse Jackson, out to pressure the RUF through its patron,
Liberian President Charles Taylor, with whom Jackson seemed to have
developed a working relationship. Jackson also met Kabbah on several
occasions with the message that he must negotiate with the rebels.

Before January 1999 this would have been a difficult sell. But following the sack of Freetown, hatred of the RUF had reached its peak among
Sierra Leoneans. Negotiations would likely reward the despised rebels
with a share of power instead of seats at the defendants' table in a war
crimes trial. Even if a settlement were reached, few Sierra Leoneans
believed the RUF could be trusted to keep its word.

Nevertheless, the international pressure proved to be insurmountable. Britain and America controlled the flow of aid. Even Nigeria,
champions of the Kabbah government, had grown weary. The Nigerian
despot, Sani Abacha, had died suddenly the preceding June—of a
heart attack, officials reported—and new leader, General Abdulsalam
Abubakar, wanted out of Sierra Leone.

In April, Sierra Leone transferred custody of Foday Sankoh to the
United Nations so he could travel to Lomé, Togo, to meet with his
field commanders. Once they were persuaded to support peace negotiations, the rebels and the government worked out a ceasefire agree-

ment. President Kabbah flew to Lomé in May for a signing ceremony on the eighteenth. Negotiations for a final peace agreement were to follow the truce's implementation a week later.

The talks in Lomé, ostensibly led by Togolese foreign minister Joseph Koffigoh, proceeded through the month of June with US ambassador to Sierra Leone, Joseph Melrose, pushing hard for a settlement from the wings. The once reclusive Foday Sankoh could be seen around his Lomé hotel where he admitted to *New York Times* correspondent Norimitsu Onishi that the RUF had committed atrocities, although not to the degree reported. Sankoh retained his "revolutionary" zeal, and claimed to be "fighting for justice," "fighting for democracy."

A peace agreement was announced in early July that called for a sharing of power. Four cabinet posts would be allocated to the RUF; Sankoh himself would head a commission on minerals and national reconciliation at the level of vice-president, but without the title to match. Sankoh and the other rebels, including Johnny Paul Koroma's AFRC, were granted amnesty for their crimes—a reward the UN refused to recognize. The RUF would transform itself into a political party and compete in elections to be held in 2001. A neutral peacekeeping force from ECOMOG and the UN would be set up to disarm all combatants.

Once again Kabbah flew to Lomé to meet Sankoh. The president and the rebel leader signed the deal on July 7 and clasped hands in wary solidarity. It was a gesture many back home in Sierra Leone would never again be able to make.

AS EVENTS LEADING to the ceasefire and the beginning of negotiations unfolded, a letter from the US National Visa Center arrived at the Mansarays'. They had been scheduled for an interview, the final step to acquiring immigrant visas. This presented a new challenge. The American embassy in Freetown had re-opened, but it no longer issued visas. The Mansarays would have to travel to far-off Abidjan if they wished to complete the process. Why not nearby Conakry? It seemed as if the US hoped to thin the ranks of applicants by erecting this formidable hurdle.

Not everyone was lucky enough to find a way to make the journey. The Mansarays, on the other hand, were fortunate to have friends who could help them. Umaru and Mabinty and their two sons said their good-byes and flew out to Côte d'Ivoire to keep their May appointment. A few hitches and several transatlantic phone calls later, the Mansarays finally got their visas. In early July they boarded an Air Afrique 747 for the twelve-hour flight to New York. Life in America would be an uncertain adventure, but at least they had escaped from the war.

Precious "green cards" in hand, the Mansarays joined the growing community of Sierra Leoneans in the Washington, DC, area. Umaru took a job in a furniture warehouse; Mabinty joined the staff of a nursing home. A yellow school bus collected Mohamed at his doorstep and deposited him safely at school. Lamini went to day care on the days his parents worked the same shift. Soon the family would be able to send money to relatives in Sierra Leone. Their dollars would help to mend the broken lives of others who couldn't get out.

> We have now started to experience our first winter here. The place is getting dark at 5:30 P.M. and the trees have lost their leaves. The color of the leaves has also changed. It is a whole new thing to us.
>
> Umaru Mansaray
> Maryland, Nov. 9, 1999

Soon after the Mansarays arrived in the US, one of their old neighbors re-surfaced back home.

> It's with great pleasure to write and inform you that I am still alive, and not dead as you may have been told....
>
> I escaped from rebel hands on the 6th June 1999, and went to Kabala through the bush. On my way to Kabala I arrived at a small village called Makakura where there was a military check-point. On my arrival at this check-point I was briefly interrogated, arrested, beaten up, and taken to the military headquarters in Kabala where I was locked up for three days for suspecting me of being a rebel or rebel collaborator. And in

fact they did not allow anybody to see me as there were over a hundred of us in that small cell. On the 4th day, however, I was released unconditionally. There is no time so suitable to write a history of my life than this one, if this is actually the end of the worst civil war in the world.

My wife, children, and grandchildren are at present languishing in Fadugu. Fadugu at present is strictly under complete rebel control....

My family and myself are looking out for humanitarian assistance from friends, organisations, religious bodies, etc. At present everything is at a standstill.

A.K. Bangura
Kabala, Sept. 25, 1999

Chapter Ten

DOUBLE CROSS

It looked for the moment as if the RUF had won. Sierra Leone's president, Tejan Kabbah, had little choice but to sign the Lomé accord. Much of his army had dissolved with the AFRC. Although the Kamajo militias would continue to be effective on their home territory, it was unlikely that they would, or could, mount a potent defense of Freetown. Nigeria, which had fought for years in Liberia and rescued the Kabbah government twice, wanted its soldiers back home. And nations of the West, champions of human rights in Europe while ignoring them in Africa, pushed hard for a settlement to silence their critics. Africa's Milosevic, Foday Sankoh, would go to Freetown—not The Hague—where he would be placed in charge of the country's diamonds.

Most Sierra Leoneans were skeptical, and bitter. "We were forced into it," Sierra Leone's ambassador to the United States, John Leigh, told the *New York Times*. "The United States went in and pushed it on us." If this were the price of peace so be it, but bygones would not soon be bygones. The saddened faces and stumps of limbs were much too present for that. People stayed put for the moment, waiting to see what would happen.

Sankoh himself remained in Lomé throughout August and September of 1999 while arrangements for his return were worked out. In an apparent show of dissatisfaction with the peace accord, a group of soldiers from the ousted AFRC junta detained a number of UN officials, journalists, and relief workers for a few days. The accord's program for disarmament, demobilization, and reintegration, during which each fighter was to surrender a weapon and enter a rehabilitation camp in return for cash, failed to make its August start date.

On October 3, Sankoh returned to Sierra Leone. House arrest in Nigeria and jail in Freetown had kept him out of action for just over two and one-half years. He had wanted to come back at the head of a triumphal convoy from the RUF stronghold in Kailahun across the country to the capital. Instead, he flew in from Monrovia with former AFRC leader Johnny Paul Koroma after receiving the counsel of Liberia's president, Charles Taylor. "We stand before you to ask for your forgiveness and a spirit of reconciliation across this country," Sankoh said at a joint press conference with Koroma and President Kabbah. "You, who we have wronged, you have every human right to feel bitter and unforgiving, but we plead with you for forgiveness." In a separate interview, however, Sankoh voiced his mistrust of Kabbah: "How can I trust him? He conspired with Abacha and others to detain a man he had signed a peace agreement with." Nevertheless, Sankoh and four other members of the RUF took up positions in a re-shuffled Sierra Leone government.

Tension also arose between Sankoh and his erstwhile ally Koroma over whose group should surrender its weapons first. Fighting between the two camps erupted in Makeni in mid-October, dampening prospects for an end to the war. A week later, the UN Security Council voted to authorize a 6,000-member force of peacekeepers in an effort to keep the process on track.

> As regards the peace talks, we are anxiously looking forward to the implementation of the accord. The disarmament, demobilisation and re-integration (DDR) of ex-combatants is in progress though at a slow pace. However, most ex-combatants do not understand the content of the DDR programme. The two rebel leaders, Cpl. Foday Sankoh and Lt. Col. Johnny Paul Koroma have currently embarked on a campaign to meet their fighters, explaining the essence of

the programme and urging them to hand in their weapons to ECOMOG and the UN peacekeeping force. Their response according to the DDR officers is very encouraging. However, the whole exercise needs time and patience.

According to reports, the 6000 strong UN peacekeeping forces will be deployed throughout the country. An advanced team of Kenyan forces [has] already arrived in the country and will be deployed upcountry (Makeni and Magburaka) while the Indian forces will be deployed in the eastern diamond mining area of Kono and Kailahun Districts though the task would be a complex one.

At the moment, it is not safe to travel upcountry. There are reported cases of attacks and harassments by the rebels on civilians in their controlled areas. Both local and International NGOs cannot carry relief foods [and] other essential items to meet the urgent needs of the civilian population for fear of being attacked. However, it is hopeful that an understanding will soon be reached by government officials, security personnel and the two rebel leaders who are now formally in Freetown to ensure that the implementation of the peace talks is carried out. It is interesting to note here that the rebel movement (the RUF) has transformed to a political party known as the RUFP (Revolutionary United Front Party). This is in accordance with the July 7 Lomé peace agreement. The party had now been issued a provisional certificate. This is another step forward for a peaceful settlement.

There is no functioning of schools in almost the entire upcountry side except for Bo, Kenema and few other places. Of course Kabala, Fadugu and any other school you know of in Koinadugu District are all closed or out of operation. Most school buildings, living quarters were destroyed or demolished and furniture removed or destroyed. I cannot tell when these structures will be rebuilt and re-furnished by the Sierra Leone government. It will require a considerable time to put all these structures back in place when the DDR exercise is completed or when the entire war comes to an end.

Currently, I am not teaching. Other teachers especially those from the North and part of the Eastern provinces are in Freetown but not teaching. The government owes us backlog salaries for a varied number of months which we have not received up till now. The permanent secretary of the Ministry of Education and other officers who were in charge of payment of these monies were apprehended by the police about 4 months ago for embezzlement. The matter is still under serious investigation....

My wife and children have asked to be remembered. We wish you and your family a happy Christmas and prosperous New Year.

Y.S. Mansaray
Freetown, Dec. 3, 1999

As THE PEACE PROCESS lurched toward an uncertain outcome, word of more casualties from the March 1999 attack on Fadugu began to filter out. Alie Mansaray, brother of Umaru and moving force behind the two men's once-prosperous partnership, had been killed by the rebels. Details had been kept from Umaru while he struggled to get his family out of Sierra Leone. Now in the US, he received the news bitterly. Over and over he had urged Alie to leave Fadugu and wait out the war in a safer place. Each time Alie had refused. He wanted to stay close to home and rebuild as much as he could. The rebels had made that impossible.

After [a December 1998] attack, rebels occupied Fadugu, and so we had to be in the bushes for over two months, eating raw fruits, and in most cases eating without salt, sleeping on cold floors, no light and no soap to wash with, and worst of all no proper clothes to wear. This condition was one of the causes of Alie's death. We returned to the town in March, and it was [during] the very March that the last attack took place where the remaining houses were burnt down, killed one healthy young man, and one old man, and amputated the arm of one woman. This was the time when Alie Mansaray and others were forced to drink the blood of an unhealthy old man, who was killed at One Mile, and that was the area where Alie and others went and hid themselves. After this, Alie managed to run away, but became seriously ill with his feet swollen and had to return to Fadugu. There was no way to take him anywhere for treatment, because there were rebels everywhere. He later died in April.

A.K. Bangura
Freetown, Jan. 18, 2000

Alie's death and Umaru's departure meant the end of the brothers' business. In good times it had been something of a stimulus for economic growth in Fadugu and Kasunko Chiefdom. As wholesalers in search of customers, the brothers provided goods and credit on generous terms to encourage others to establish retail businesses in bush villages not routinely served. Their own sales increased as a result, and the standard of living for a number of new entrepreneurs gradually began to rise. The war brought an end to this nascent progress. Now its promise for future development in a time of peace would be lost.

THE FIRST CONTINGENT of United Nations peacekeepers, several hundred soldiers from Kenya, arrived in Freetown on December 1, 1999. Their task would be herculean. No sooner had they hit the ground than they came under verbal attack. Although he had agreed to such a force at Lomé, Foday Sankoh denounced the foreigners, saying it was up to Sierra Leoneans to solve their own problems. His top field commander, Sam Bockarie, flatly refused to cooperate with the UN. Attempts by the peacekeepers to disarm the rebels "will be met by force," he said.

The arrival of the peacekeepers brought a new acronym, UNAMSIL (United Nations Mission in Sierra Leone), to the lips of Sierra Leoneans. The old standby ECOMOG would soon fade from the lexicon as Nigeria began to withdraw the bulk of its troops. A few thousand would remain as part of the UN force, augmented by the Kenyans and others to come from Ghana, India, and Zambia. Given the UN's hostile reception by the rebel side and the realization that the withdrawal of

ECOMOG would diminish both the numbers and expertise of "neutral" forces, UN Secretary-General Kofi Annan quickly asked the Security Council to increase the number of peacekeepers from 6,000 to 11,000.

The UN's mission was far from clear. How much authority did it have to make the parties comply with the peace agreement? Could its soldiers use force against recalcitrant combatants? Would UN members contribute enough money and equipment to sustain the operation? One thing was certain: If peace was to be established, the fighters would have to surrender their weapons. To this end the UN directed much of its effort. But as 1999 faded into 2000 only 6,000 fighters had been disarmed and even fewer weapons, 4,542, collected. With an estimated 45,000 combatants at large—10 to 15,000 RUF and AFRC fighters plus as many as 25,000 Kamajo and other civil defense forces and a few thousand loyal government soldiers—this was a small beginning.

The pace picked up a bit in January and February as another 12,000 turned themselves in. The operation was marred, however, by several incidents in which rebels forcibly resisted UN troops, especially in the Kailahun and diamond-rich Kono districts that the RUF still controlled. In February, the rebels' leader, Foday Sankoh, was further embittered by his deportation back to Freetown from South Africa for violating a UN travel ban on members of the RUF. Sankoh claimed to have been seeking medical treatment, while others accused him of selling diamonds.

In spite of the shaky beginning of the process, some Sierra Leoneans chose to look toward a peaceful future.

> My home village [Petifu] is totally burnt down and there is no place for me in Fadugu as well. There are only very few houses in Fadugu and all the few remaining ones are at the extreme corners of the town. In about two years more I will be retired, and I have a large family with some of the children still attending school, so it will be nice for me to have a house myself. I have already made arrangements for the making of mud blocks and some of my friends, children, and relatives are ready to provide most of the local materials.... After putting up

the building at Fadugu, I then have to go home [to Petifu] and concentrate on my agricultural project work together with my sisters and brothers and build a house in the village....

Schools are running in the [Koinadugu] district with a lot of constraints. In Fadugu town, all the furniture were damaged by rebels, and of course there are no books and any other school materials. However, teachers, pupils and the local community are doing their level best to keep the system going.

R.U.F. rebels are still in Fadugu, but they seem to be in good terms with the civilian population, but most of us are still hesitant to stay together [with them]. All what we want is the total disarmament so that normal life can return to our areas.

I will be leaving for Kabala early next week and will come back to Freetown in two months to come and talk to you. My wife, children and grandchildren are asking here for special greetings to you and wife.

A.K. Bangura
Freetown, March 30, 2000

IN FRANCE they call it "cohabitation" when the president from one political party is forced by the electorate to govern with a prime minister from another. Uneasy as it may be, the jousting in France that results from such a condition is always confined to the verbal. In Sierra Leone, the cohabitation produced by the Lomé accord could easily turn to violence. None of the parties—the government, the rebels, Kamajo, and former AFRC junta soldiers—trusted the others, and to make the situation even more difficult, Sierra Leone had no money of its own to resettle the country. President Kabbah succinctly addressed the problem in an end-of-March interview with *West Africa*:

In my discussions with the former rebel leaders their one reoccurring demand is: 'What is in it for our men?' I am also under pressure from the victims of the war, particularly the amputees. They say to me: 'We don't have arms anymore, we cannot work for ourselves.' They want to know what is going to be provided for them. There are many people whose factories,

> livelihoods and properties were destroyed. These are people who no longer have the means to earn a living. Because of the war, we have not received money as a government. We have not received a single penny from the mines that are our single major source of revenue…. We have massive security problems that have to be financed and we have our people looking to us to reduce their deprivation. But there is nothing. It is hard.

The European Union and the World Bank agreed to finance the disarmament. Britain had contributed some £65 million over the past three years and pledged another £17.5 million to support the peace process. The US pledged $55 million in new assistance and an additional $65 million of debt forgiveness. But on the ground in Sierra Leone where the only reliable currency was a gun, those numbers were mere abstractions. If the peace agreement was to be fully implemented, the UN troops might well have to use force.

The peacekeepers in their blue berets were woefully equipped for such a mission. Absent from those contributing troops were the world's major powers—the United States, Britain, France, Russia—who could easily have mustered elite units armed with the latest weapons and support. "The best peacekeeper is a well-trained soldier," UN Secretary-General Kofi Annan told the *New York Times*. "We would have liked to see some of the governments with capacity—with good armies and well-trained soldiers—to participate. But they are not running forward to contribute to this force. So we have to take the forces we get."

UN peacekeepers were drawn from some of the world's poorest nations. They lacked training, were lightly armed—rifles, but no tanks and artillery—and generally came from the lower reaches of each country's army. No presidential guards were represented here. These were expendable troops whose presence at home would scarcely be missed. Few had experienced combat, and none knew much about Sierra Leone. To think that they could stand up to the battle-hardened RUF seemed the height of fancy.

The build-up of untested UN forces coincided with the withdrawal of ECOMOG. Ever since the war began the wily Nigerians had helped to keep the RUF from power. Their departure presented the rebels with a fresh opportunity that they wasted no time in seizing. In the first week of May 2000, the rebels reversed the disarmament process. They captured a number of UN soldiers, killing one, and took their weapons away. By the end of the week more than 500 UN soldiers were believed to be hostages of the RUF. Some of those had attempted to move into the diamond district of Kono, whose gems, mined by the rebels, were a primary source of revenue the RUF was unwilling to give up. In Freetown, Foday Sankoh claimed the missing were merely lost in unfamiliar terrain. His men, he said, "are helping to look for them." Then Sankoh himself disappeared.

> Things have not yet calmed down in my country. There was a peace/civil demonstration about 3 weeks ago [May 8] which was organised by the Civil Society Movement and parliamentarians at RUF rebel leader Foday Sankoh's residence in which 20 people were shot dead by Sankoh's special bodyguards, and several other people were wounded who are currently being hospitalised at the Connaught Hospital....
>
> The fighting has actually resumed. The government forces together with the civil defence militia [Kamajo] and the paramilitary forces [former AFRC soldiers] are currently pursuing the rebels and are making successful gains according to report from defence headquarters.
>
> I reliably learnt that the rebels have burnt the military barracks at Teko in Makeni and are committing all sorts of atrocities in their strongholds, burning peoples' homes, schools and other important buildings in Makeni town. Fadugu, Kamabai, Binkolo are part of their strongholds. I cannot tell what might have taken place in those towns and their surrounding villages. There is no vehicular traffic at the moment in those areas and no one is moving to those upcountry homes.
>
> To be candid, it would make more sense for me and my family to leave Sierra Leone if at all we had the opportunity to do so within the shortest possible time. I have very little sleep or rest whenever I assess the current situation and events in the

country. Recent developments here have left me in a state of dilemma.

The UN forces are here to give help to the people of Sierra Leone to settle their crisis provided there is cooperation and sincere commitment to the peace process. But there is yet that lack of trust and confidence amongst the stakeholders and even amongst the civil populace.

Y.S. Mansaray
Freetown, May 28, 2000

THE DEMONSTRATION at Foday Sankoh's house that Y.S. Mansaray described had started as a peaceful protest against the breakdown of the peace process. The people of Freetown blamed Sankoh, and thousands converged on his house chanting and singing for an end to the fighting. As the noisy demonstrators pressed against the compound's walls, some began throwing rocks. UN troops assigned to security tried to reason with the crowd when, suddenly, shots rang out. Civil defense soldiers and dissident former AFRC members, known as the West Side Boys, had infiltrated the demonstration and opened fire on the house. Sankoh's bodyguards shot back, scattering the demonstrators in panic. Amid the chaos Sankoh slipped away.

Meanwhile fighting between government forces and the rebels broke out in the area of Rogberi Junction along the Freetown–Makeni highway, some eighty miles from the capital. Britain dispatched 800 paratroopers, ostensibly to secure Freetown's Lungi Airport and evacuate foreigners, but their role quickly expanded to securing the capital itself. The UN scrambled to beef up its forces from the current 8,700 to the authorized 11,000 with fresh troops from Bangladesh, India, and Jordan. But with many of its forces detained by the rebels and no mandate to join the fighting, it seemed unlikely that, absent a change of mission, the UN could do much to stem the violence.

Sierra Leoneans took some comfort from the arrival of the British troops. Although their numbers were small and they would not be attached to the UN, the paratroopers were first-rate soldiers, well-trained and armed with up-to-date weapons, including helicopter gunships, night vision equipment, and support from seven ships of the Royal Navy just off the coast. The US, on the other hand, refused to send its soldiers. Despite President Clinton's apology to Rwanda for failing to intervene during the slaughter of nearly one million of its people in 1994, the memory of dead American soldiers being dragged through the streets of Mogadishu, Somalia, in 1993 seemed to have enervated his administration when it came to Africa. Instead, the US offered to transport other countries' forces for three times the commercial airline rate and to send Jesse Jackson back to the region, even though his persistent advocacy of negotiations with Foday Sankoh made him unwelcome in Freetown.

The day after Sankoh dropped from sight, UN troops abandoned Masiaka, forty-seven miles from Freetown, when they ran out of ammunition. A UN spokesman said the peacekeepers were regrouping into defensive positions around the capital and would now fight to defend themselves. Former AFRC leader Johnny Paul Koroma and most of his soldiers rallied to the side of the government, vowing to battle the rebels. Doubtful civilians began to hope for the return of ECOMOG.

A week after the ill-fated demonstration at Foday Sankoh's house, Indian peacekeepers in Kailahun persuaded the rebels to release eighteen hostages. The following day mediation by Liberia's Charles Taylor won freedom for another 139. Again thanks to Taylor, 80 more emerged from captivity soon afterward. But the rebels themselves continued to fight.

On Wednesday, May 17, their leader re-appeared in Freetown. Arriving at his house in the early morning, apparently to retrieve items left behind, Foday Sankoh was captured by neighbors, stripped naked, and paraded to the home of Johnny Paul Koroma. Koroma, in turn, handed him off to the Sierra Leone army, and Sankoh was whisked away in a British helicopter. He had apparently never left the city during his nine-day disappearance. A short while later, RUF members serving in the government were arrested.

The breakdown of the peace accord prevented all but one Fadugu correspondent from getting letters out of the country. Y.S. Mansaray, still languishing in Freetown, reported that A.K. Bangura remained in Kabala unable to travel. "The rebel forces are still occupying the towns of Lunsar and Makeni. One could only get to and from Kabala by air through the use of helicopters which are strictly controlled by the UN."

Despite his often unemotional, war correspondent's delivery, Mansaray's growing despair still surfaced among stoical words.

> As regards the peace process, it has been on 'pause' since May 8 when 21 people were shot dead by rebel guards of RUF leader Foday Sankoh during a peaceful march at his residence....
>
> I look forward to you for help in order to get me and my family out of Sierra Leone at the moment. Those who have the opportunity to do so have left the country. I believe you have by now been able to contact Umaru Mansaray and some [other] persons from Fadugu living in the US to find out how they were sponsored and what type of visa they received....
>
> Hope your wife and son are both well.... I pray and hope that some day we shall all be able to stay together as one family.
>
> Y.S. Mansaray
> Freetown, July 25, 2000

AN EMBARRASSED UNITED NATIONS had gotten the remainder of its hostages back at the end of May. Nearly all of them had gained their release through the auspices of Charles Taylor. The obvious ploy would have been for the RUF to demand freedom for Foday Sankoh in return for giving up the hostages. While there was some talk of this, the rebels never seriously pursued such an exchange. With Sankoh in detention and field commander Sam Bockarie holed up in Monrovia after quarreling with Sankoh at the end of 1999, it seemed clearer than ever that ultimate control of the rebels rested with Taylor.

The means of that control had initially included the supply of weapons, training, occasional manpower, and the cover of Liberian territory, but in the latter nineties Taylor's stealthy assistance to the "revolution" yielded to blatant commercial enterprise based in the illicit diamond

12/5/14

Dear David,

Here's a review copy
of Black Man's Grave
for you. Thanks for
giving it a look.

Best wishes,
Gary Stewart

trade. Gems mined in Sierra Leone by the RUF flowed out through Liberia. Arms purchased abroad with diamond profits flowed back into Sierra Leone the same way. Operatives connected to Taylor bought the gems and imported the arms. According to a report on Sierra Leone diamonds published by Partnership Africa Canada, "In 1988, before Liberia erupted, the country exported US $8.4 million worth of diamonds, including a great many smuggled Sierra Leonean diamonds. In 1995, when Liberia lay in ruins and economic activity was almost non-existent, it exported US $500 million worth of diamonds."

Many of those diamonds came from Sierra Leone and from the UNITA rebels in Angola, who also financed their war with diamond profits. In the words of Partnership Africa Canada, "Where diamonds were concerned, Liberia had become little more than a fencing nation, creating fictive mines as cover for the immense laundering of diamonds smuggled from other nations, mainly Sierra Leone." Although Taylor did not become president of Liberia until 1997, he and his NPFL controlled most of the country throughout the nineties.

In July of 2000 the UN Security Council imposed a world-wide ban on the purchase of Sierra Leone's diamonds until a method of identifying the stones' origins could be devised. The ban lasted until October when, with help from Belgium's Diamond High Council, Sierra Leone instituted a certification system. The broader diamond industry, through a series of meetings known as the Kimberley Process, also moved to stem the trade of so-called "conflict diamonds" by developing a method of tracking gems from mine to jewelry store. The resulting system was voluntary, however, and relied chiefly on the veracity of the participants.

With international pressure mounting, Liberia's Charles Taylor began to react. His intervention to gain the release of the hostage UN peacekeepers had been a constructive first step. Then in August of 2000 he purchased three full pages in *West Africa* to rebut charges that he dealt in illegal arms and diamonds: "My government categorically denies all of these allegations and challenges anyone to produce one shred of evidence." As for the rebels in Sierra Leone, he wrote, "we do admit to a relationship with the RUF, which is no secret. However, we reject any notion that that relationship is based on pecuniary gains from diamond dealing and gun running." He pledged that his government supported "a speedy return to the implementation of the Lomé Accord" and called for an immediate ceasefire.

A panel of experts established by the UN Security Council sharply disputed Taylor's claims. The panel's report, submitted at the end of 2000, "found unequivocal and overwhelming evidence that Liberia has been actively supporting the RUF at all levels, in providing training, weapons and related matériel, logistical support, a staging ground for attacks and a safe haven for retreat and recuperation." It fingered a Lebanese businessman living in Monrovia named Talal El-Ndine as the operation's paymaster.

The report accused Burkina Faso of collaborating with Liberia to move arms to the RUF in exchange for diamonds. It named a certain Ibrahim Bah, a resident of Burkina who sometimes uses the alias Ibrahima Baldé, as a key liaison between Monrovia and Ouagadougou. The report also linked international arms trafficker Victor Bout of Tajikistan to the complex web of clandestine dealings that originated in Sierra Leone's diamond pits.

Following the September 2001 attacks on the United States, Western nations suddenly became far more interested in the illegal trafficking of Sierra Leone's diamonds than they had ever been before. *Washington Post* reporter Douglas Farah traced gems from Sierra Leone through Liberia to Osama bin Laden's al Qaeda network. Citing unspecified "intelligence sources" and various others not named, Farah reported that in September of 1998 Ibrahim Bah arranged a visit to Liberia by alleged bin Laden adviser Abdullah Ahmed Abdullah. According to Farah, Abdullah met the RUF's Sam Bockarie "to discuss buying diamonds on a regular basis." A few weeks later, two other members of al Qaeda met Bockarie "taking him $100,000 in cash and receiving a parcel of diamonds in an introductory deal." A subsequent investigation by Global Witness, a London-based human rights organization, confirmed Farah's reports.

These events appeared to be the beginnings of an attempt by al Qaeda to empty its bank accounts, which could be frozen or seized by governments, and convert the cash to diamonds, which could be easily hidden and reconverted to cash when necessary. They also help to explain the RUF's reluctance to surrender control of Sierra Leone's diamond areas.

Meanwhile, on the ground in Sierra Leone, where the brunt of Charles Taylor's actions often fell, conditions seemed to be improving, almost imperceptibly.

> Since May this year I have not been able to contact any of my
> friends or relatives in Fadugu or Kabala. The highway from
> Freetown to these areas [is] still closed. I got information that
> after the rebels were repelled from Kabala about eight weeks
> ago, some of them (the rebels) returned and occupied the
> township of Fadugu. I also reliably learnt that some of the
> inhabitants have abandoned the town and are currently taking
> refuge in neighbouring villages or farms which is making life for
> them very, very difficult and miserable. The town, I also learnt,
> is very bushy and filthy causing serious health hazards for those
> who are staying there right now. I also get reports of deaths
> due to malnutrition, hunger and diseases in the township and
> its environs. There is complete change (physically, socially,
> culturally, economically, etc.) on the life of the community
> people. The entire situation has caused us fear of insecurity and
> uncertainty about our future and those of our children. It will
> not be an easy task any longer for some people to resettle or
> rebuild their homes. This is a plain truth. The war has caused
> permanent setbacks on some people who doesn't even know
> about politics or crime.
>
> The peace process is still on course anyway. There is at the
> moment no report of fighting country-wide. It is also relatively
> calm in Freetown. Some of the fighting forces are gradually
> handing in their weapons and registering themselves for the
> Disarmament, Demobilization & Re-integration (DDR)
> program.

A.K. Bangura has still not been able to come to Freetown and I have not been able to contact him. I am sure whenever he comes, he will call you on the phone. Please send me your phone number.

I have submitted an entry for the DV-2002 [United States] Diversity Visa Lottery. If selected, I need your support and blessing.

Y.S. Mansaray
Freetown, Oct. 25, 2000

Chapter Eleven

SIMMER DOWN

While Charles Taylor drew rein on the RUF, a chagrined United Nations gradually discovered its backbone. The initial plague of disorganization and the embarrassment of hostage peacekeepers had passed for the moment. Now the UN built up its forces in Sierra Leone toward a new goal of 13,000, and the soldiers themselves turned aggressive.

In a bold strike in mid-July 2000, UN troops aided by helicopter gunships liberated 222 peacekeepers and 11 military observers who had been surrounded by RUF rebels for more than two months in Kailahun. A few days later another UN contingent attacked a group of the West Side Boys, who had been harassing traffic on the Freetown–Makeni road near the town of Masiaka. The change in tactics led more combatants to join the disarmament, demobilization, and re-integration program.

It seemed increasingly clear that disarray among the rebels had sapped the movement's will. In August, with Foday Sankoh and many of his lieutenants in jail and Sam Bockarie in Monrovia now claiming to be a businessman uninterested in the war, the RUF, or at least a faction of it, put forth a little known fighter named Issa Sesay as its new leader. Sesay, it was said, belonged to the Sankoh faction that had won a power struggle with Bockarie at the end of 1999. Who he really was or what sort of clout he carried among hard-core rebels was difficult to tell.

Further evidence of the rebels' changing fortunes came at the hands of the British. Near the end of August the West Side Boys captured eleven British soldiers. The circumstances were mysterious to say the least, since the captives belonged to a unit in the country to train a new Sierra Leone army. How had they managed to stray into rebel territory? Did they mean to attack the West Side Boys? Where were their Sierra Leonean trainees?

Negotiations won the release of five soon after they had been captured, but the rebels refused to give up six others. Britain flew in more paratroopers as negotiations stretched on over two weeks. Then, at dawn on September 10, British forces raided the rebel camp in the Occra Hills near Masiaka and freed the remaining captives. Twenty-five rebels and one British soldier died in the action. The British captured another eighteen rebels and turned them over to the Sierra Leone government.

British and UN accomplishments were briefly tarnished by more problems within the leadership of UNAMSIL, the UN mission in Sierra Leone. The military commander, Major General Vijay Jetly of India, traded criticism with his deputy, General Mohammed Garba, and the special representative of the UN secretary general, Oluyemi Adeniji, both of whom were Nigerian. The dispute ended with India pulling out of UNAMSIL altogether. Jetley and Garba were replaced by Kenyan Lieutenant General Daniel Opande and Nigerian Major General Martin Luther Agwai.

On November 11, during negotiations in Abuja, Nigeria, the government of Sierra Leone and the RUF agreed to a new ceasefire. As part of the deal the RUF promised to allow UN peacekeepers to take up positions in the diamond mining areas. But RUF negotiators were headed by another unknown, one Jonathan Kposowa, not purported new leader Issa Sesay. Whether or not Kposowa had the backing of Sesay and whatever other rebel leaders were left would remain to be tested on the ground back home. Nevertheless, it was the first significant contact between the two sides since the Lomé accord broke down in May.

What most Sierra Leoneans are yearning for at the moment is the disarmament, demobilization and re-integration of the rebels or ex-combatants into society, but they are still holding out in the bushes in trying to destroy civilians. The major road between Freetown to Makeni and Kabala is open to traffic use, but the rebels have mounted several checkpoints (about 20) making it difficult for vehicles or people to travel freely. And most unfortunately the government hasn't up till now been able to extend its authority to rebel controlled areas.

Parliamentary and presidential elections which were due this February couldn't be held due to a number of factors one of which is lack of funds to conduct the elections and voter education exercises, and above all a larger portion (about 80 percent) of the country is still being held or controlled by the rebels who have not disarmed or given themselves up to the government.

> Y.S. Mansaray
> Freetown, Feb. 27, 2001

In March of 2001 Sierra Leone would begin its eleventh year of war. Ahmad Tejan Kabbah's term in office would expire just before that sorrowful anniversary. Although the elections before peace movement had carried him to the presidency five years earlier, this time around there was little stomach and no money to conduct a new poll. Parliament voted unanimously to extend its own term and that of the president for six months.

THE CEASEFIRE in Sierra Leone seemed to be holding even as fighting briefly spread into Guinea and Liberia. RUF rebels attacked Guinean troops on their own soil just east of Kailahun. Guinea in turn attacked the RUF inside Sierra Leone, while Guinean-backed Liberian rebels crossed the border to raid bases of the Liberian army. Meanwhile the UN Security Council voted to impose stiff sanctions on Liberia if it didn't end its support for the RUF.

Ten years of war with little to show but the destruction of the country, the incarceration or exile of its more radical leaders, and growing international pressure on its sources of money and arms, brought the remaining RUF leaders to a new understanding. "We are in a stalemate," a rebel spokesman named Gibril Massaquoi told the *Washington Post* in April. "We are not defeated but we can't take power, and therefore the people will suffer if the war continues. We are now ready to struggle politically, not militarily."

It is doubtful whether the rebels will give up the diamond mines without putting up stiff resistance. Another problem is the Charles Taylor factor who continues to aid the rebel outfit and whose interest in our diamonds to [salvage] his beleaguered economy could also be crucial in finding a solution to the present crisis.

Revelations from several meetings in the recent past between the RUF fighters and UNAMSIL have indicated that the RUF is willing to disarm, demobilize and re-integrate into society but are contemplating attacks from the civilian populace when taking into account the atrocities and sufferings they inflicted on innocent people. And moreover a large number of people are questioning the sincerity of the rebels taking into account their past records.

However UNAMSIL as a neutral body has always assured the fighters of their safety and security after they shall have handed over their weapons. Moreover adequate lectures are given by the National Commission for Disarmament, Demobilization and Re-integration (NCDDR) officers on the entire process which is catering for their needs and security. His excellency the President Ahmad Tejan Kabbah in his broadcasts and tours to the provinces has also been appealing to the fighters to give up their weapons in the best interest of themselves and the nation ... and has always assured them of their safety and security....

All we are asking for is a life of peace so that we can get back on our feet and live a decent life. We as Sierra Leoneans should collectively work together with the international community, the United Nations, ECOWAS, OAU to lead Sierra Leone out of this hole in order to save the majority of innocent people. A change of attitude is a good start on this long road to recovery for all Sierra Leoneans.

My best regards and best wishes of Easter.

Y.S. Mansaray
Freetown, April 2, 2001

At the beginning of May, UN sanctions on Liberia, including a ban on travel by government officials and a tightening of embargoes on arms and diamonds, went into effect. The squeeze on Liberia choked the RUF. On May 2, following more talks in Nigeria, the rebels and the government announced a new deal to end the war. A joint committee including UNAMSIL, the RUF, and the government was established to oversee disarmament of the rebels and the civil defense militias. The government agreed to certify the RUF as a political party. Fighting was to cease immediately.

Even before this latest agreement a lull could be detected. People moved more freely, although subject to RUF "taxes" at each of its impromptu checkpoints. Communication began to improve a bit. And news of Fadugu, cut off for many months, began to filter out once again.

It's a little over one year now since I last spoke and wrote you. I hope you received my last letter together with group pictures of some members of my family....

My wife, children, and grandchildren are all with me in Kabala. They all left Fadugu over one year ago when the rebels [resorted] to raping, looting, and committing other human atrocities. Presently, there appears some calm in the area [of Fadugu], but people no longer trust the rebels. People can only feel free and safe after they are disarmed. There are very few houses in the town. People are beginning to return to the town, but most of them sleep in palm thatched huts, and broken houses. This then means that my family and myself will be in Kabala till the situation returns to complete normal life.

As you may have heard in the interview with our minister of education [on] the BBC last week concerning the payment of teachers' monthly salaries, I have not been paid for the past six months, and I still have no hope of getting any pay soon. We are almost like refugees in Kabala. CRS [Catholic Relief Services], MSF [Médecins Sans Frontières] and other NGOs supply us some food items some times. We are managing up things. We hope that very soon the war will be over.

I have already acquired land in Fadugu to put up at least a four-room house building.... Over 9/10 of the houses in Fadugu are destroyed, but the people are determined to rebuild their homes after disarmament.

Schools are functioning in Kabala under difficult conditions. There are very few or no school learning materials and no furniture. Pupils/students have over grown in age and size. My twin sons will be twenty years old in November and they are still in JSS III [third year of junior secondary school, the equivalent of ninth grade], because the West African Examinations Council refused to conduct examinations in all rebel controlled areas in the country.

A.K. Bangura
Kabala, April 16, 2001

In a public ceremony in Makeni near the end of May, the RUF attempted to demonstrate its good faith by releasing some four hundred child soldiers. The children, most of them teenagers but some as young as six, were taken to rehabilitation camps, the first stop on a road to re-integration which for the lucky ones would see them reunited with their families. In July, a tough, well-armed contingent of Pakistani peacekeepers moved into the heart of diamond territory for the first time—although for the moment their presence did little to disrupt illicit mining by both the rebels and Kamajos. By the middle of August a UN spokeswoman claimed that 16,000 combatants had turned in their weapons.

I am … happy to inform you that peace is gradually returning to our beloved country Sierra Leone, and people have started returning to their various homes from their various places they sought refuge during the war. The disarmament exercise is in full progress. In fact the disarmament team will be in Kabala on the 15th of this month to disarm all the warring factions in the district. Generally, the country is now calm….

People have started returning to Fadugu, but are faced with the problems of shelter, food, clothing and medicine. The rains are now heavy in Sierra Leone, and people sleep in their palm thatched huts and in broken houses….

My wife is at present in Fadugu with two of my grandchildren to make a small inland swamp rice farm.

A.K. Bangura
Kabala, August 5, 2001

IT SEEMED ONCE AGAIN that an end to the war was at hand. Despite their disorganization, inexperience, and muddled rules of engagement, the 13,000 and counting UN peacekeepers had profoundly altered conditions on the ground in Sierra Leone. The promise of peace had been lost before, but this time there was reason to hope. Like A.K. Bangura, many Sierra Leoneans started to think of life after the fighting.

The rebuilding of Fadugu and Kasunko Chiefdom, if it was to come at all, would be hindered by a scarcity of leaders. Paramount Chief Alimamy Fana II had died at the hands of the rebels. Leadership fell to the chiefdom speaker who would act as regent until after the war. In multi-ethnic Kasunko, a chiefdom ruled by Limba paramount chiefs, the current speaker and now regent was the Mandingo section chief, Alhaji Abu Bakar Mansaray. Alhaji's own house had been burned by the rebels in 1998, so he fled to Freetown to await the day when he would preside over Fadugu's resurrection. But as the fighting dragged on his health declined. He died in Freetown on August 26, 2001, around the age of eighty-five. New, as yet unknown, leaders would now have to take up the task.

Even as death summoned its leader Fadugu showed signs of rebirth.

> I am happy to let you know that rebels have been disarmed in
> the entire Koinadugu District, and people are returning to the
> district. Fadugu is now totally free of rebels.
>
> I am presently in Freetown to fight for school materials,
> because schools will reopen on September 10, but there is
> nothing at all to start with. Of course, as for Fadugu, there is
> only one [school] building that appears to be in a fairly good
> condition, so we are appealing to NGOs for assistance. We are
> desperately in need of help. Teachers have no place to stay and
> no furniture or school learning materials. UNICEF has just
> provided some text books and exercise books to start with.
>
> A.K. Bangura
> Freetown, Sept. 6, 2001

The trauma of eleven years of war was cause enough to be self-absorbed, still many Sierra Leoneans felt the impact of September 11. Some paused from the grim task of repairing their own lives to commiserate their friends in America.

> I was completely shocked and sorry to learn on Tuesday,
> September 11, 2001 [of the] tragic events, about the series of
> co-ordinated and devastating attacks on the United States … by
> international terrorists.
>
> On my personal behalf and that of my family, we are offering
> our sincere and profound condolences [for] what had happened
> to the victims and the families of those involved and to the
> entire people of America.
>
> Y.S. Mansaray
> Freetown, Sept. 17, 2001

A new war was in the making, but Sierra Leone's seemed over. People began to emerge from the bush where they had hidden from homegrown terror. They ventured back into Fadugu in search of friends and family and to see if any belongings survived. Old correspondents, who had been missing and thought dead, began once again to write.

The peace process is really working well in Sierra Leone. Vehicles especially commercial ones are now moving freely from Freetown to Kabala.

Life is a little bit normal in Fadugu these days. It is only the accommodation part of life that is difficult because of the very many burnt houses. The rebels who were staying in the area have been disarmed so the place is peaceful at the moment.

There was no magic I employed in getting myself safe and survived during the war. I always escape from the RUF with my family by running into the bush whenever we gather information about their arrival in the township of Fadugu. We used to spend sleepless nights in dark places with snakes and wild animals just to get ourselves away from the rebels. It is really a miserable story to narrate fully. Praise be to the peacekeepers for we are now sleeping well with no hesitation....

Our house in Katimbo [an area of Fadugu] was brought down to grass-root level by the rebels. There is no way to get it erected for now for there is no finance. We are managing with the family to live in thatch houses. There is [a] plan to start rebuilding the house during the dry season.

Peter S. Kamara
Fadugu, Sept. 20, 2001

[During] all the 12 or more attacks in and around Fadugu, I and family were around. We moved from village to village, bush to bush, saving our lives.

The worst out of all the rebel attacks were the government gunships and its bombardments on innocent civilians. The Alpha Jet, as it was called [used by ECOMOG], was far better. But with all that we were safe by God. Feeding and medicines were our biggest problem. Cassava became our major food and some wild fruits in the bush also became our food and medicine.

Fadugu's destruction and the plight of its residents is difficult to explain as relatives drive relatives away from themselves either because of food, noise, sleeping place or overcrowd[ing]. Here no talking, only actions, afraid of being heard by the rebels or seen by gunships.

As for [Fadugu's] destruction, starting from the first house in One Mile to the last house in Katimbo, were all burnt down both by rebels or the government jet or gunships.

Presently we are thankful, movement and the rights of civilians are now observed. The news you hear really sounds good about the peace process. Vehicles including government bus are all moving freely in Koinadugu and other districts. The old market system has started with all sorts of items.... Fadugu is really coming back to its old life.

Farming is going on fine. Children and youths play as they used to play at night. Men, women move for poyo [palm wine] or visiting friends. Some people have started rebuilding their houses with the old burnt zinc [roofing] which do not last long....

As for myself, really all I want now is [to do] trading. It is the only way to make money and rebuild my house and start planning for the future.

> Sylvanus S. Kanu
> Fadugu, Dec. 4, 2001

By December 14,000 weapons and nearly half a million rounds of ammunition had been collected by UN peacekeepers. The goal of disarming the estimated 45,000 fighters appeared to be within reach. Refugees who had fled to Guinea and Liberia began to trickle warily across the border to Sierra Leone. Freetown gained some elbow room from the steady drift of people back to the countryside. Day by peaceful day Sierra Leoneans began to trust that there would be no more fighting.

My wife and children are always eager/anxious to hear from you and so they were extremely happy when they saw your letter, especially after the September 11 attacks in America.

I am happy to let you know that disarmament of ex-combatants in the Koinadugu District is over, and this means that there is no R.U.F. rebel again with gun in the district. The district officer, paramount chiefs, top civil servants are all expected to go/return to the district to start work next week. The police and the Sierra Leone army are in the district to maintain law and order. The entire district is now calm and peaceful.

As for Fadugu many people have returned there to start rebuild[ing] their life, destroyed and damaged homes. I mean people are doing everything to forget the past and plan for the future. Already the usual marketing day on Sundays has started and people from surrounding villages, from Makeni, Kabala, etc., go there every Sunday to buy and sell, even though there [are] no houses. They sleep in palm thatched huts, open air, churches, broken houses, etc.

This is how I have planned to start the building work [on my house]. Immediately schools close for Christmas on 14th December 2001, my family and myself will go to Fadugu to start the mud block making, make arrangement for sticks, sand and stones. Hopefully, between February and March, work on raising the walls will begin, and I am sure by the end of March that may have been completed. The most difficult side of the whole exercise is that of iron sheets (zinc), roof nails, cement, boards. Of course the use of the other materials such as paint, white wash, etc. will follow later. The house itself is a four room house and a two room back yard house. I will send you the plan of the house as soon as I get it.

A.K. Bangura
Kabala, Nov. 20, 2001

PEOPLE ALSO BEGAN to think about rebuilding national political institutions. The Kabbah administration still governed nearly one year beyond the expiration of its constitutional term. President and parliament had been elected in 1996 by a minority of Sierra Leoneans brave enough to risk a trip to the polling place, if indeed there was one in their area. The approaching peace would make it possible to conduct wide-open political campaigns and full-scale elections.

The move towards new voting had been given a boost in September when several RUF leaders—but not Foday Sankoh—were released from detention to help organize former rebels into a political party. In November, 250 delegates representing government, political parties (including the RUF), and civic groups convened a "national conference" at Kingtom in Freetown's west end. Delegates adopted some twenty-five resolutions concerning government reform and the conduct of fair elections.

In Fadugu, where the citizens had seen their representative in parliament repeatedly imposed upon them by Siaka Stevens and his All People's Congress, an emerging group of young leaders moved to seize the initiative.

> [We held] a meeting in which we were to present an aspiring candidate in the person of Tejan A. Mansaray for the forthcoming general elections who is to represent the people of Kasunko Chiefdom in the House of Parliament. We the descendants of Kasunko are very much determined to have a son of the soil to represent us in parliament.
>
> It is a fact that the people of Kasunko have suffered far too long or way behind in the history of parliamentary representation. I am sure with concerted efforts, determination, co-operation, good will and with support we will succeed in our goal.
>
> I quite believe we have friends who are willing and determined to assist in the process of any development of Kasunko. We have quite a number of well-educated sons and daughters of the chiefdom and we only need to choose good and honest persons to put them in positions of trust. The future really depends on a new generation, i.e. young leaders.
>
> Y.S. Mansaray
> Freetown, Nov. 9, 2001

Mansaray also reported that for the first time since Fadugu was destroyed in 1998, the townspeople came together to celebrate Christmas and New Year's. A team of UNAMSIL peacekeepers traveled down from Kabala for a friendly Christmas Day football (soccer) match against Fadugu's best (1-0 UNAMSIL). In the evening "a hectic dance (disco) was staged at the Fadugu N.A. [native administration] court barrie to entertain the youths for peace and reconciliation. The celebrations continued till New Year's Day making everybody happy once more after many years of not coming or celebrating together."

ON FRIDAY, JANUARY 18, 2002, across the Sierra Leone River from Freetown, President Kabbah declared the war to be ended. Accompanied by Ghana's president, John Kufuor, and assorted dignitaries from the UN, Nigeria, Liberia, and even Libya, Kabbah set fire to a pile of 2,991 confiscated weapons in a symbolic immolation of the tools that had destroyed the country. "The forthcoming electoral process will test our patriotism, our determination to put armed conflict behind us, to renounce violence as a means of bringing about political or any other change in this country," Kabbah told the assembled crowd. "If we really appreciate peace, we should live and practice peace."

The scene repeated in provincial capitals. At Makeni, RUF leader Issa Sesay and thirteen of his commanders surrendered their weapons and joined in setting fire to another pile of guns. More cleansing rites were held at Kenema in the east and in the southern city of Bo.

Where the country would go from here defied prudent prediction. Time and money could repair ruined villages. Scarred minds and broken bodies would take much longer to heal. But for the first time in eleven years, all the people of Sierra Leone could live without fear of the rebels.

> The making of mud blocks started on the 27th December, 2001, and over 2000 mud blocks have been made. I only need less than 1000 more.
>
> The construction of the building itself will start this month and by the end of March the building of the walls would have been completed. I have bought some boards and sticks. Now

the main and most important thing is that of [obtaining] zinc and cement....

The population in Fadugu has over grown. Most of the people have returned, but there is no proper dwelling place. My wife and four of the children together with me and two of my grandchildren are living in one small room....

Greetings to you and family.... The war is totally finished and we are all safe and happy.

A.K. Bangura
Fadugu, Feb. 16, 2002

Epilogue
Taking Stock

The end of combat seems to call for a reckoning, as if the horror of the battlefield can somehow be neatly tallied. The ravaged countryside, where this war claimed most of its victims, produced few reliable body counts. Fadugu's Alie Mansaray died among friends who could at least give him a respectful burial; so many others perished alone in the bush or were consigned to their graves by strangers. Various estimates put Sierra Leone's dead at some 50,000–70,000, but such figures are simply guesses.

Among the living, Sierra Leonean refugees in Guinea reached close to half a million around the time of the 1999 Lomé accord when their numbers were thought to be greatest. By 2001, more than 334,000 had registered as displaced persons inside Sierra Leone. Perhaps one million others, like many residents of Fadugu, ran away to the bush to evade the rebels and could never officially register their status. As in the case of the number of deaths, such a figure is simply a guess.

A study of internally displaced persons conducted in 2001 by Physicians for Human Rights revealed that slightly more than nine percent of women and girls had been subjected to some form of war-related sexual violence. By extrapolating, PHR estimated that 50,000 to 64,000 had suffered such abuse. These numbers would only increase if the rest of the population could be accounted for. Letters from Fadugu, for example, indicate that many women and girls there were sexually assaulted. Of those in the study who reported the identity of a perpetrator, 60% blamed the RUF. Fewer cases of sexual violence were attributed to the AFRC and other remnants of the Sierra Leone army

(28%), and fewer still (2%) to ECOMOG. No one in the study claimed to have been sexually abused by soldiers of the civil defense militias or UN peacekeepers, although Human Rights Watch reports it has documented several such cases.

Another study, this one by a German humanitarian organization called Christ End Time International, found that some 3,750 had been maimed by the bloodthirsty swing of a matchet. Among them 656 had both arms and both legs chopped off. Another 400 were children. How many more died as a result of their amputations is impossible to tell.

Dealing with the perpetrators of this madness presented a difficult challenge. In keeping with the Lomé accord the Kabbah administration had pardoned all combatants. Since the accord broke down in less than a year, should the pardon be allowed to stand? In any case, the UN refused to recognize the pardon when it came to "international crimes of genocide, crimes against humanity, war crimes and other serious violations of international humanitarian law." Furthermore, with the war over the government would need to lift the state of emergency it had declared thus losing the legal authority to detain Foday Sankoh.

Justice minister Solomon Berewa solved this latter problem in March of 2002 by charging Sankoh with murder in connection with the deaths that occurred outside his house during the demonstrations of May 2000. A trial was put off indefinitely when no lawyer qualified to practice in Sierra Leone could be found to represent him. Beyond that, Sankoh's mental state raised the question of his fitness for trial. Former US ambassador to Sierra Leone, Joseph Melrose, told a Washington audience in September of 2001 that Sankoh suffered from "serious psychological problems; he hears voices and talks to people that no one else sees or hears."

At President Kabbah's request an international effort to bring to justice those who committed war crimes and crimes against humanity in Sierra Leone began to take shape. The UN and Sierra Leone's government negotiated an agreement to set up the independent Special Court for Sierra Leone to sit in Freetown. By the end of 2001 nearly all of the $16 million needed for the Court's first year of operation had been raised from UN members. The chief prosecutor, a former judge advocate in the US army named David Crane, began work in August of 2002. The Court's eight judges, two from Sierra Leone and six from abroad, took the oath of office in December.

To aid the process of reconciliation and enhance the historical record, the negotiators at Lomé had included a provision in the peace agreement that called for the establishment of a truth and reconciliation commission. Parliament enacted the necessary legislation in early 2000, but the breakdown of the peace accord prevented its implementation.

With fighting finally at an end, the seven-member Sierra Leone Truth and Reconciliation Commission was launched officially in July of 2002 under the chairmanship of Dr. Joseph C. Humper, bishop of the United Methodist Church of Sierra Leone. In December, staff members began taking statements from all who wished to tell their stories. Still, management problems and the public's confusion about the commission's purpose hampered its progress. Many Sierra Leoneans felt the Truth and Reconciliation Commission and the Special Court were working together. Others appeared reluctant to talk to the commission for fear their testimony would be used against them in the Special Court—this despite assurances to the contrary from both bodies. An association of people who had suffered amputations threatened to withhold its cooperation from the commission until the government began to address the problems of the war's most visible victims.

Despite its fitful beginnings the Truth and Reconciliation Commission gathered support as 2003 unfolded. In April the commission started to hold public hearings in major towns around the country. The sessions drew large crowds to hear former fighters and their victims tell stories of horrific encounters.

As regards the combatants themselves, UNAMSIL registered more than had been thought to exist. Earlier estimates may have been wrong, or perhaps a few civilians converted temporarily to take advantage of the reintegration allowance. Whatever the case, by December of 2002, 56,750 had surrendered, among them 6,845 children. UNAMSIL collected 2 million rounds of ammunition along with 27,664 weapons. This latter figure would appear to be low when compared to the number of combatants, a worrisome peculiarity. Still, thanks to the more than 17,000 UN troops and observers from 31 countries, a general feeling of security had returned to Sierra Leone.

NEAR THE END OF 2001, the year that traded war for peace, the National Electoral Commission produced a plan for conducting elections. The following January, parliament passed much of that plan into law. Seats in parliament would increase from 80 to 124 to be allocated according to a "district block" system, since no current census existed to draw constituencies based on population. The Western Area, which includes Freetown, would be split into two electoral districts. These along with the twelve administrative districts in the countryside would each be allotted eight seats to be filled from party lists in proportion to the number of votes each party received. The remaining twelve seats were reserved, as before, for paramount chiefs, one to be elected from each administrative district.

The electoral commission began conducting voter registration even before the new law was passed. By March some 2,276,518 had registered, nearly three quarters of a million more than had been able to sign up in 1996.

Polling day, May 14, 2002, proceeded with ten parties on the ballot seeking seats in parliament and nine candidates for president. The RUF nominated Pallo Bangura, a cabinet minister during the RUF's brief participation in the Kabbah government, as its candidate for president in place of Foday Sankoh whom the electoral commission declared ineligible. Under the watchful eyes of UNAMSIL and other international observers, eighty-one percent of those registered peacefully cast their votes, despite some logistical foul ups and a few cases of probable fraud. At the end of the day President Kabbah had overwhelmed his challengers, capturing seventy percent of the vote. The APC's Ernest Bai Koroma polled twenty-two percent to finish a distant second. The RUF received a scant two percent.

As you might have heard over the radio the past general elections (presidential and parliamentary) were peaceful and fairly conducted. [Fadugu's] Tejan A. Mansaray was a parliamentary candidate under the SLPP for Koinadugu District and was elected to parliament together with five other candidates under the same party and two others under the APC party. This means the SLPP won six seats and the APC won two seats in Koinadugu District.... Out of the fourteen districts including the Western region of Sierra Leone there are 112 seats. The SLPP won 83 seats, APC won 27 seats, and PLP (Peace and Liberation Party of former junta leader Johnny Paul Koroma) won 2 seats.

Kasunko Chiefdom [is] lucky to have a son of the soil to represent us in parliament for the next five years. Generally speaking, we are all happy to have Mr. Mansaray in parliament and it is our earnest desire and hope that he would be able to lead us and live up to expectations as we are prepared at all times to give him our support for better development in our chiefdom.

Y.S. Mansaray
Fadugu, May 26, 2002

One troubling note in an otherwise remarkable achievement concerned Sierra Leone's military and police. Since their members would be called upon to maintain order on election day, they cast votes separately on May 10. Vote tallies later showed that "large numbers" of them supported Johnny Paul Koroma, not their commander-in-chief. This revelation was sure to test the country's nerves, especially after UNAMSIL withdrew.

President Kabbah alluded to this in his inaugural address at the opening of the new parliament July 12. Citing the country's various episodes of military intervention, he lauded the people's resistance to them. "I am convinced," he declared, "that democracy is now fully entrenched in our society."

I was in Freetown on July 12 to witness the state opening of the second session of parliament and the inauguration of President

Ahmad Tejan Kabbah. The occasion was also witnessed by
President Obasanjo of Nigeria, Lansana Conte, of Guinea,
Kufuor of Ghana, Yahya Jammeh of the Gambia, vice-president
of Liberia, special representative of the United Nations to
Sierra Leone, foreign diplomats, journalists, party stalwarts,
religious and tribal leaders, men and women of all walks of life,
cultural dancers, musicians, etc. It was indeed a very colourful
and memorable occasion. I wish I had something to record the
events.

The general elections of paramount chiefs for parliament
were conducted on June 10, 2002. They proceeded without
any problems. There were two candidates for Koinadugu
District (P.C. Alhaji Alimamy Lahai (incumbent) of Sinkunia
Chiefdom and P.C. Magba II of Kondembaia, Diang
Chiefdom). P.C. Alimamy Lahai emerged the winner and he
is now representing Koinadugu District for a second term of
office.

As for the paramount chief elections in Kasunko Chiefdom,
no date has yet been scheduled by government. However, there
are secret campaignings going on by intending candidates.

Y.S. Mansaray
Fadugu, July 20, 2002

THE HOLDING OF ELECTIONS to fill vacant chieftancies—sixty-four
chiefs had been killed by rebels or died from other causes during the
war—was part of the government's overall effort to extend its administrative authority. Civil servants returned to their posts over the course
of 2002, and the Sierra Leone Postal Service resumed operations
upcountry.

The police, in the process of re-training by UN and Commonwealth
personnel and bolstered by new recruits, established at least a tentative
presence in each district. By the end of 2005 the target of 9,500 police
deployed throughout the country appeared to be within reach. Only
4,000 were fully trained, however, leaving much work still to be done.
The new army, being trained by British soldiers, began to deploy its

troops with an eye to replacing UNAMSIL as the guardian of security, but budgetary constraints and lack of infrastructure and equipment hindered progress. Troop strength stood at around 13,000 by the end of 2005 with reductions to 10,500 envisioned by 2007. Efforts to re-establish the judiciary gained less traction. Poor pay and working conditions discouraged qualified Sierra Leoneans from accepting positions on the bench.

MEANWHILE, in Fadugu, life was gradually returning to normal.

> There is presently a new mosque [having] been constructed by Bangladesh (UNAMSIL), and a … dispensary [has] been constructed by Christian Children's Fund. The site for the [old] market area was the place used for the construction of the mosque. The construction of the [new] market is in the pipeline using another site. There is also a good plan that Christian Children's Fund wants to repair the water pipe system in the whole township. The Roman Catholic Mission also wants to build a secondary school for the Fadugu community. The repairing program for the old D.E.C. [government primary school] buildings is now in progress. We are expecting fast development in Fadugu in order for us to forget about the destruction done by these aimless rebels.
>
> We now have a new paramount chief in Kasunko Chiefdom. He was duly elected on the 18th December 2002. His former name was Mr. Alfred B.S. Kamara but now called P.C. Lamin Baio Serry III.
>
> Peter S. Kamara
Fadugu, Jan. 11, 2003

Even before the new chief, the new mosque, and the various government and NGO undertakings, A.K. Bangura reported: "I have gone far with my building project. Already, my family and myself now manage to live there…. I was living or staying in a small room which is so small that we decided to move to my new house, though it is not yet complete." As for his ancestral village of Petifu, Bangura wrote that "Petifu was destroyed more than Fadugu…. It is extremely pathetic. I only hope I will be able to do something before the situation gets worse."

Y.S. Mansaray wrote to tell of assistance for the town from Catholic Relief Services, which was offering sheets of corrugated metal roofing, nails, and cement for those who could come up with the other essentials, like blocks and boards, for rebuilding. "My elder brother and myself have taken on the challenge: to reconstruct one of our family houses under [the auspices] of this same organization." Y.S. also considered contesting for the position of Mandingo section chief but eventually withdrew in favor of a family elder. Instead, he resumed teaching at Fadugu's government primary school where he was eventually promoted to headmaster.

The other Mansarays, brothers Alie and Umaru, were no longer around to rebuild. Alie's decision to stay in Fadugu cost him his life and triggered a cascade of misfortune. Just weeks before he died in April of 1999, Alie's wife, Salimatu, gave birth to their third son, Karifala. Alie's death left Salimatu to fend for herself, Karifala, and second son Sarabaio in the rebel-infested area around Fadugu (the couple's oldest son, Mamadu, remained with relatives in Freetown). By the end of 1999 the two boys had fallen ill from the effects of hiding in the bush. Both died before the new year.

As is customary among Mandingos, a widow becomes the wife of one of her dead husband's relatives; in Salimatu's case this was one of Alie's cousins. She bore him twins in June of 2002. One of the babies died during a difficult birth that sent Salimatu into a coma. She died one month later. The remaining twin died in January 2003.

In the United States, Alie's brother Umaru sent money home to help maintain his mother, Alie's son Mamadu, and several other relatives. He attended nursing school at night, completing his training in early 2003. His new credential afforded Umaru a broad choice of jobs in the health care industry with its promise of better pay. Upon Umaru's graduation his wife Mabinty followed the same path to nursing school. The family expanded in 2004 with the birth of a baby girl. The following year Umaru and Mabinty and their (now three) children left their cramped, rented apartment for a spacious house of their own.

Fadugu's industrious Mammy Thor had managed to stay a step ahead of the RUF, departing Fadugu and then Makeni just before the rebels had overrun them. She wound up in Freetown beside her husband, the regent chief Alhaji Mansaray, as he lived out his final days. Around the same time she lost one of her twins, Adama, to sickle-cell anemia. Her oldest daughter, Yeabu, newly returned from America, fell ill and died soon after. Despite her grief, Thor pressed on, returning upcountry to her house in Makeni while she awaited the reconstruction of her Fadugu buildings.

For other victims of the war and those who fought it, the future looked more uncertain. The amputees would never be able to resume life as they had known it. Most would likely be unemployable and would look to the state for help. Few former fighters seemed anxious to go back to the farm. Many of them wouldn't even go home for fear of retribution. Projects under the reintegration program kept most ex-soldiers occupied temporarily, but the government would be hard-pressed to provide training and jobs over the longer term. In the best of times only a small fraction of Sierra Leoneans had ever earned regular wages. What would 57,000 ultimately get for giving up their AK-47s?

The president attempted to answer that question in his inaugural address by outlining an ambitious recovery program. Key elements would include the rehabilitation of agriculture, road repair and construction, rebuilding the health care system, and restoration of the nation's economy. In addition the president called on members of parliament to help stamp out corruption: "I entreat you to regard corruption as a national security issue. It is that serious." For the country to succeed this time around, however, the government would need to move past the lofty talk to prove to the people that it was an ally not an enemy, that it could make meaningful improvements in their lives, that the wealth of the country would be used for the common good

◆ ◆ ◆

DIAMONDS, the country's main source of wealth, remained an area of concern. Responsibility for security in the diamond mining areas passed into government hands in August of 2004, even as large numbers of ex-combatants remained there to search illegally for precious stones. The Kabbah administration struggled to establish a coherent licensing and enforcement system that would stem the illicit trade, increase benefits to the local people, and still insure a steady flow of revenue to the national treasury. The discovery of diamonds at Kamakwie, in the north, further stretched the government's ability to supervise the use of its natural resources.

Sierra Leone's new diamond certification system, instituted in 2000, would discourage smuggling only within the broader framework of an international certification system. The Kimberley Process, the diamond industry's attempt to establish such a scheme continued, somewhat unsteadily, to develop. Following the issuance of the first "Kimberley certificate" by Israeli diamond merchants in January 2003, the "process" grew to include some forty countries. No common certificate was agreed upon, however, leaving each country to come up with its own. Kimberley countries adopted a procedure for peer review whereby each member could request examination of its compliance with the process, but the absence of mandatory monitoring appeared to leave the door open for continued illicit trade. Still, diamond certification seemed to be paying off for Sierra Leone. The scheme, coupled with an end to the fighting, boosted the value of the country's diamond exports from a negligible amount in 1999 to $76 million in 2003 and $116 million in 2005.

Another area of concern for Sierra Leone was the instability of its neighbors. A coalition of anti-Charles Taylor groups known as Liberians United for Reconciliation and Democracy (LURD) had begun launching attacks in north-western Liberia in July of 2000. Three years later LURD forces held a sizeable amount of Liberian territory and threatened to take Monrovia. The fighting sent a new wave of Liberian refugees across the border to Sierra Leone and offered new employment opportunities for former RUF soldiers who wished to shoulder arms once more. Likewise, the September 2002 beginning of rebellion in nearby Côte d'Ivoire was said to involve Sam Bockarie and other fighters from Sierra Leone.

Two incidents inside Sierra Leone also added a measure of disquiet. In January 2003, several armed men attacked a military installation on the outskirts of Freetown in what appeared to be an attempt to seize weapons. The police fingered Johnny Paul Koroma; although they arrested a number of people at his house, Koroma himself escaped. The following year, in November, forty-five prisoners escaped from Freetown's Pademba Road Prison, including several members of the RUF and the West Side Boys.

IN MARCH 2003, the Special Court handed down its first indictments. Foday Sankoh and three other leaders of the RUF, Sam Bockarie, Issa Sesay, and Morris Kallon stood accused of war crimes along with former AFRC junta members Johnny Paul Koroma and Alex Tamba Brima. In addition the Court indicted former deputy defense minister and leader of the Kamajo militias, Samuel Hinga Norman. Five of the seven were quickly rounded up, but Bockarie and Koroma remained at large.

Sankoh appeared before a Special Court judge on March 15, in the town of Bonthe on Sherbro Island nearly 100 miles down the coast from the pressure cooker capital. The rebel leader who had appeared trim and vigorous during the Lomé talks in 1999, looked confused and disheveled, like one of Freetown's deranged vagrants, as an attendant delivered him to the proceedings in a wheelchair. He never uttered a word and seemed not to understand what was happening. The performance cast doubt on Sankoh's competence to stand trial. His death at a Freetown hospital on July 29, 2003, settled the matter.

Unlike the charges against Sankoh and his cohorts, which had long been anticipated, the indictment of Hinga Norman, the sitting minister of the interior, caught most Sierra Leoneans by surprise. Norman and his Kamajo militias had fought on the side of Sierra Leone's democratically elected government. Without them it seemed likely that the rebellion's leaders would be sitting in State House instead of the

Special Court's lockup. Sierra Leoneans, most of whom had welcomed the Court's establishment, now began to reconsider. Many in the ruling Sierra Leone People's Party—but not President Kabbah—openly condemned Norman's arrest. The United Kingdom's ambassador to Sierra Leone during the war years, Peter Penfold, joined in the criticism. "What message does Sam Hinga Norman's arrest send to others who are prepared to fight for the cause of peace and democracy?" he asked in a letter to colleagues. Norman supporters in the UK and the United States started to raise money for his defense.

Nearly three months after Norman's arrest, Chief Prosecutor Crane announced the indictment of another prominent warrior, President Charles Taylor of Liberia. Taylor, said Crane, bore "the greatest responsibility for war crimes, crimes against humanity and serious violations of international law."

It turned out that Taylor had been the first to be charged, back on March 7, but the indictment was sealed with the hope that he could be captured by surprise when he traveled outside of Liberia. Such an opportunity presented itself on June 4, as Taylor flew to Ghana for talks with the rebels who threatened to oust him. The Special Court conveyed a warrant for his arrest to Interpol and the Ghanaian government, but Taylor returned home unimpeded. The Ghanaians had been reluctant to arrest a sitting head of state, particularly one of their neighbors. "Unsealing the indictment at this particular moment," said Ghana's foreign minister, "has not been helpful to [Liberia's] peace process."

In the meantime, at the beginning of May, Taylor's forces killed the fugitive Sam "Mosquito" Bockarie. Initially thought to be a ruse to enable Bockarie to evade prosecution, the killing was later verified when Liberia handed the body over to Sierra Leone for identification. It seemed likely that Taylor had simply eliminated a source that could deliver incriminating testimony against him.

A similar fate was said to have met Johnny Paul Koroma. Both Koroma's wife and the Special Court's chief investigator announced that Koroma had been murdered in Liberia at the end of May. If true, his death would deprive whatever dissidents remained in Sierra Leone of a powerful rallying figure. As of this writing, no body had been produced for verification.

Following Koroma and Bokarie, Taylor underwent his own transition. With rebels entrenched in parts of the capital and US warships looming on the horizon, he resigned as president on August 11, 2003. The ex-president departed for exile near Calabar in southeastern Nigeria, a perch that, for the moment, kept him beyond the reach of Sierra Leone's Special Court. Once again the UN would mount a peacekeeping force in an attempt to duplicate in Liberia the success it had won next door.

ON OCTOBER 5, 2004, the Truth and Reconciliation Commission issued its final report—what could reasonably be called the most candid and constructive document ever produced in Sierra Leone. If the essence of its several thousand pages, collected in five volumes, could be captured in a few words, they would be these: Bad governance caused the country's civil war; good governance would prevent it from happening again.

"The RUF and its supporters were responsible for the greatest number of human rights violations during the conflict period," the commission found, but AFRC, civil defense, and government troops also bore responsibility. The commission noted "an astonishing factional fluidity among the different militias and armed groups" and found the composition of fighting forces to be strikingly similar: "impressionable, disgruntled young men eager for an opportunity to assert themselves, either to ensure that no harm was done to their own people, to fight against perceived injustice, or for personal and group aggrandisement." The country would have to find more meaningful roles for its young people to stem the tide of alienation.

While young men were estranged, the commission found that women were objects of prejudice. They bore the brunt of sexual crimes during the war, and in times of peace "gender inequality is entrenched in all spheres of social, political and economic life by discriminatory laws, customs, traditions and practices." The government should repeal such laws the commission said. Women too must be allowed to join society's main stream.

The commission observed that Sierra Leone's current constitution "devotes more space to taking away the rights of citizens than to ensuring their respect." It recommended that a new constitution be written through a broad consultative process. But, the commission urged, whatever constitution, old or new, the death penalty, which successive governments have used "to eliminate political opponents," should be abolished.

Noting that "there is not a single reference to the word 'ethics' in the Constitution," the commission pleaded for the cultivation of "a culture of ethics and service." Corruption was rampant at all levels, it said, and "successive governments have failed to meet the basic needs of most Sierra Leoneans, particularly those outside of Freetown." Parliament, judiciary, civil service, security services, chieftaincy, natural resources— the commission recommended reforms in every area of Sierra Leone's administration. Where the money and the will to make such sweeping changes would come from was an open question.

While the Truth and Reconciliation Commission took testimony and wrote its report, Sierra Leone's volatile neighbor slowly regained its equilibrium. A week after Charles Taylor flew into exile in August of 2003 Liberia's principal factions signed a peace agreement in Accra. On October 14 an interim leader, businessman Gyude Bryant, took office in Monrovia. In December, the first of Liberia's more than 100,000 combatants handed in their weapons to peacekeepers from unmil, the United Nations Mission in Liberia. Disarmament and the gradual reintegration of soldiers into civilian life smoothed the way for the return of constitutional rule and elections, in October and November of 2005, for a new government. The first woman to be elected president of an African country, Ellen Johnson Sirleaf, took her oath of office on January 16, 2006.

Johnson Sirleaf's inauguration was bad news for Charles Taylor. During a March meeting in Abuja, the new president asked Nigeria's President Obasanjo to hand Taylor over for trial at Sierra Leone's Special Court. Soon afterward Obasanjo agreed.

Charles Taylor returned to a ravaged Monrovia in the afternoon of March 29, where UNMIL police promptly arrested him. He had briefly evaded Nigerian authorities in a dash for freedom, but an alert border guard stopped him as he tried to enter Cameroon near the northern town of Gamboru. Why Taylor would travel nearly 700 miles north in Nigeria instead of heading less than 30 due east to cross into Cameroon remained unexplained. The magazine *New African*, citing anonymous sources, claimed that the Nigerian government had collaborated in the attempted escape. Whatever the intrigues, Taylor found himself in custody on Liberian soil. An UNMIL officer read him his rights then escorted him to a helicopter for a short flight to Freetown and the Special Court's jail.

With Taylor locked up, discussions turned to the question of what his presence might mean for peace in the region. Liberia's Ellen Johnson Sirleaf, among others, called for his transfer to The Hague. Officials there agreed to host a trial if another country would incarcerate Taylor in the event of a finding of guilt. Britain agreed to assume that responsibility. Soon afterward the UN Security Council authorized the arrangement. On June 20, 2006, Charles Taylor was flown to the Netherlands where he would be tried for war crimes by the Special Court for Sierra Leone, sitting at the International Criminal Court.

The restoration of stability in Liberia meant that UNAMSIL's plans for withdrawing its forces from Sierra Leone could proceed as planned. Troops had begun to leave late in 2002, reducing the number of peacekeepers to 11,500 at the end of 2003 and 4,000 in December 2004. By the end of 2005, all but a handful had gone. UNAMSIL was no more.

AFTER ELEVEN YEARS OF WAR and five more of UN tutelage, Sierra Leone had regained its independence. Whether the second epoch would better the first was far from being assured. In its report the Truth and Reconciliation Commission bluntly stated that "proper governance is still an imperative, unfulfilled objective in Sierra Leone. Corruption remains rampant and no culture of tolerance or inclusion in political discourse has yet emerged. Many ex-combatants testified that the conditions that caused them to join the conflict persist in the country and, if given the opportunity, they would fight again. Yet, distressingly, the Commission did not detect any sense of urgency among public officials to respond to the myriad challenges facing the country."

In his first report since the dissolution of UNAMSIL the UN's Kofi Annan offered a further assessment. Noting a "worsening youth unemployment situation," "no improvement in water and power supplies," high cost of essential commodities, and "persistent fuel shortages," he wrote: "There is a general perception that the Government's inability to deliver basic services or respond to the needs of the population is due to corruption and mismanagement of public resources, and this has become a source of tension."

As seasonal rains washed over the land in mid-2006, the Kabbah administration staggered toward the exit. It had weathered some of the country's most tumultuous times and could, perhaps, be forgiven for its apparent lethargy. Elections were set for the early months of 2007. New leaders might soon come to power, bringing with them new hope for the future. Y.S. Mansary may have expressed the thoughts of many in the broader society when he wrote, "I am hopeful that in the next coming years Fadugu will have a different outlook and will be a convenient place to live."

Notes

20 "Plan of a Settlement...": Porter, 20n2.

20 160 languages and 40 dialects...: Curtin, 289–98.

23 Freetown's population...: *Sierra Leone Yearbook 1965*, 33; *Handbook of Freetown*, 1.

46 For every three children born...: UNICEF, 140. UNICEF's estimate for 1990 was 302 under five deaths per 1,000 births.

46 "taken out of the country...": Koroma, 30.

46 "I can take comfort...": Stevens, 370.

47 According to one estimate...: Reno, *Corruption and State Politics*, 137.

50 One veteran of the 1977 campaign...: conversation with author John Amman.

56 Bangura's "stranger" was author Gary Stewart.

59 "Sierra Leone's shops...": *West Africa*, Mar. 27, 1989, 475.

59 "Solutions to our socio-economic...": Ibid.

61 Charles Taylor's escape: *Boston Globe*, July 31, 1990, 1.

62 An incensed Charles Taylor...: *West Africa*, Nov. 19, 1990, 2875; Dec. 3, 1990, 2955.

62 According to Sierra Leone's...: Koroma, 141.

65 "Those of us in the army...": *New African*, Nov. 1999, 42–46.

66 March 23, 1991, was the twentieth anniversary of the two attempts to assassinate Siaka Stevens—a foiled coup d'etat that resulted in prison time for Foday Sankoh.

68 A November visitor was author Gary Stewart.

68 "virtually now over": *West Africa*, Nov. 18, 1991, 1940.

70 "New wine...": Ibid., Nov. 4, 1991, 1850.

70 Momoh's and Strasser's radio addresses: Ibid., May 11, 1992, 788.

71 Strasser's radio address following the coup's success, "Fellow citizens…": Ibid.

72 Strasser's account of his days before the coup: Ibid., June 15, 1992, 1002.

73 In a rare interview…: Ibid., July 13, 1992, 1184.

78 "tailoring supplies…": De Beers, "De Beers and the Diamond Industry," January 1998, 14, quoted in Smillie, *Heart of the Matter*, 22.

80 "From a high…": Smillie, *Heart of the Matter*, 42.

80 In addition to leading the Amal Movement, Nabih Berry has been president of Lebanon's National Assembly since 1992.

82 "planned to fight…": *New African*, Nov. 1999, 44.

83 According to … Ibrahim Abdullah: Abdullah, "Bush Path," 203–35.

88 "carefully compiling a picture…": Richards, "Anarchists or Catalysts?," 265.

89 families of organized crime: Berkeley, 15.

97 In a follow-up letter: *West Africa*, Jan. 30, 1995, 138.

97 according to … Ibrahim Abdullah: Abdullah, "Bush Path," 217.

97 "We are democrats…" and additional quotations on page 97: Revolutionary United Front.

99 Accounts vary about exactly how much money Executive Outcomes was to receive in Sierra Leone. The $2000–$7000 figures come from Rubin, 47. The $1.8 million figure comes from Hirsch, 38. *See also* Cilliers and Mason.

100 "scores of citizens…": *West Africa*, May 15, 1995, 750.

101 "to sincerely pursue…": Ibid., May 11, 1992, 789.

105 "young men who refused…": Ibid., Oct. 23, 1995, 1634.

105 "They're ripping out tongues…": *Daily Telegraph*, Dec. 16, 1995, quoted in *West Africa*, Dec. 25, 1995, 1994.

105 "By unleashing…": Koroma, 208.

106 "force the NPRC…": *West Africa*, Jan. 22, 1996, 103.

106 "Our commitment to restore…" and additional quotation on p. 106: address by Julius Maada Bio, State House, Jan. 17, 1996.

114 Kamajo is often spelled Kamajor but is correctly pronounced ka-ma-jo. In addition to the Kamajo militias, which were the best known of Sierra Leone's civil defense forces, the *Tamaboroh* hunters of the north, *Donzos* in Kono District, *Gbethis* in central Sierra Leone, and *Kapras* to the west, all did battle with the RUF.

120 The peace agreement worked out in Conakry was entitled "ECOWAS Six-Month Peace Plan for Sierra Leone, 23 October 1997–22 April 1998." The plan called for the Kabbah government to be "restored to office on 22 May 1998," thus making it a seven-month plan in reality.

123 Information about the diversity visa lottery comes from Divine, 393–402. Early variations of this program began in 1987.

125 Civilian casualties: *West Africa*, Feb. 16, 1998, 224.

125 "make this a new...": Associated Press dispatch, *Tallahassee Democrat*, Mar. 11, 1998, 5A.

135 The slain rebel commander was S.A.J. Musa, a former NPRC member who had joined the RUF.

136 "We wanted the people...": *West Africa*, Feb. 1, 1999, 55.

137 Casualty figures: *New York Times*, Jan. 26, 1999, A1.

138 Number of refugees along the Guinea border: U.S. Committee for Refugees.

140 "The time has come...": *New African*, April 1999, 21.

141 Foday Sankoh interview: *New York Times*, June 18, 1999, A4.

145 "We were forced into it...": Ibid., June, 5, 2000, A14.

146 The initial disarmament, demobilization, and reintegration package called for the payment of $150 in leones when a fighter surrendered and another $150 worth of leones three months later when the fighter had completed some form of re-education for a return to society.

146 "We stand before you...": *New African*, Nov. 1999, 46.

146 "How can I trust him...": Ibid.

146 In addition to Sankoh, the following members of the former RUF/AFRC junta joined the government: Mike Lamin (minister of trade and industry), Pallo Bangura (minister of

energy and power), Peter Vandy (minister of lands, housing, country planning and the environment), and A.B.S. Jomo-Jallo (minister of tourism and culture).

149 "will be met by force,": *West Africa*, Nov. 29, 1999, 28.

150 Number of fighters disarmed and weapons collected: Ibid., Jan. 24, 2000, 17.

150 Another 12,000 turned themselves in: Ibid., Mar. 13, 2000, 10.

151 President Kabbah's statement: Ibid., Apr. 3, 2000, 12.

152 "The best peacekeeper…": *New York Times*, May 11, 2000, A10.

153 "are helping to look…": Associated Press dispatch, *Tallahassee Democrat*, May 5, 2000, 3A.

155 The government said it had arrested 120 people including cabinet ministers Mike Lamin, Pallo Bangura and Peter Vandy along with RUF spokesman Eldred Collins.

157 "In 1988…": Smillie, *Heart of the Matter*, 46.

157 "Where diamonds were concerned…": Ibid., 45.

157 "My government categorically…": *West Africa*, Aug. 21, 2000, 18–20.

158 "found unequivocal and overwhelming…": United Nations Security Council, *Report of the Panel of Experts*, 33.

158 Douglas Farah's reporting: *Washington Post*, Nov. 2, 2001, A1.

158 Global Witness confirms Farah's reports: Global Witness, especially 41–65.

165 Sierra Leone's constitution empowers parliament to postpone elections, six months at a time, if the country is at war on its own territory.

166 "We are in a stalemate…": *Washington Post*, Apr. 14, 2001, A1.

168 16,000 combatants: Ibid., Aug. 23, 2001, A21. It should be noted that following the breakdown of the Lomé accord in May 2000, the reintegration payments of $300 per combatant were suspended. In October 2001, the reintegration payments resumed at the reduced rate of Le300,000 ($162) plus $15 transportation for each combatant.

172 Amount of weapons and ammunition collected: Malan, 51.

173 Parliament had voted to postpone elections for an additional six months on September 12, 2001. *See also* note for page 165.

175 "The forthcoming electoral process…": *West Africa*, Feb. 4, 2002, 19.

179 Number of deaths: Gberie, 2; International Crisis Group, *Sierra Leone After Elections*, 1; Malan, 13; *New York Times*, Jan. 19, 2002, A6.

179 Number of refugees: Physicians for Human Rights, 1n.1; U.S. Committee for Refugees.

179 Number of people subjected to sexual violence: Physicians for Human Rights, 2–3 and 53.

180 Additional information on sexual violence: Human Rights Watch, 27–28.

180 Number of amputees: *West Africa*, July 15, 2002, 21.

180 "international crimes…": United Nations Security Council, *Seventh Report of the Secretary-General on the United Nations Observer Mission in Sierra Leone*, par. 7.

180 Remarks by Ambassador Joseph Melrose are quoted from *Friends of Sierra Leone Newsletter*, Spring 2002, 6, which paraphrases Melrose.

181 The Special Court's original eight judges were Sierra Leoneans George Gelaga King and Rosolu John Bankole Thompson. They were joined by Renate Winter from Austria, Geoffrey Robertson of England, Nigerian Emmanuel O. Ayoola, Benjamin M. Iteo of Cameroon, Canadian Pierre Boutet and Hassan B. Jallow of Gambia.

181 In addition to Bishop Humper, other Sierra Leonean members of the Truth and Reconciliation Commission were Justice Laura A.E. Marcus-Jones, Professor John A. Kamara, and teacher and administrator Sylvanus Torto. They were joined by Yasmin Louise Sooka of South Africa, Ajaaratou Satang Jow from Gambia, and Canadian William Schabas.

181 Numbers of fighters surrendered and weapons and ammunition collected: United Nations Security Council, *Sixteenth Report*

of the Secretary-General on the United Nations Mission in Sierra Leone, par. 19 and 28; *Thirteenth Report of the Secretary-General on the United Nations Mission in Sierra Leone*, par. 13.

182 Number of voters registered: United Nations Security Council, *Thirteenth Report of the Secretary-General on the United Nations Mission in Sierra Leone*, par. 24.

183 Military and police votes for Johnny Paul Koroma: United Nations Security Council, *Fourteenth Report of the Secretary-General on the United Nations Mission in Sierra Leone*, par. 12; International Crisis Group, *Sierra Leone After Elections*, 9.

183 "I am convinced...": Inaugural Address by His Excellency Alhaji Dr. Ahmad Tejan Kabbah, Parliament Building, July 12, 2002. President Kabbah was sworn in for his second term on May 19, 2002, however his inaugural speech was given at the opening of parliament nearly two months later.

184 Police staffing: United Nations Security Council, *Twenty-seventh Report of the Secretary General on the United Nations Mission in Sierra Leone*, par. 31.

185 Army staffing: Ibid., par. 30.

187 "I entreat you...": Inaugural Address by His Excellency Alhaji Dr. Ahmad Tejan Kabbah, Parliament Building, July 12, 2002.

188 Statistics on Sierra Leone's diamond exports from Levin and Gberie, 10.

189 In addition to Hinga Norman, two other members of the CDF, Moinina Fofana and Allieu Kondewa, were indicted. The three were being tried together in one proceeding. Surviving RUF members, Sesay and Kallon were being tried jointly with a later RUF indictee, Augustine Gbao. The case of AFRC member Alex Brima was joined to that of later AFRC indictees Brima Bazzy Kamara and Santigie Borbor Kanu. As of this writing in mid-2006, the three trials were still in progress.

190 "What message...": *West Africa*, May 12, 2003, 5.

190 "the greatest responsibility...": *Washington Post*, June 5, 2003, A22.

190 "Unsealing the indictment...": Ibid.

191 "The RUF and its supporters...": Sierra Leone Truth and Reconciliation Commission, vol. 2, chap. 2, par. 115.

191 "an astonishing factional fluidity...": Sierra Leone Truth and Reconciliation Commission, vol. 2, chap. 1, par. 36.

191 "gender inequality...": Sierra Leone Truth and Reconciliation Commission, vol. 2, chap. 3, par. 319.

192 "devotes more space...": Sierra Leone Truth and Reconciliation Commission, vol. 2, chap. 3, par. 66.

192 "to eliminate...": Sierra Leone Truth and Reconciliation Commission, vol. 2, chap. 2, par. 415.

192 "there is not a single...": Sierra Leone Truth and Reconciliation Commission, vol. 2, chap. 3, par. 219.

192 "successive governments...": Sierra Leone Truth and Reconciliation Commission, vol. 2, chap. 3, par. 248.

192 100,000 combatants: United Nations Security Council, *Tenth Progress Report of the Secretary-General on the United Nations Mission in Liberia,* par. 21.

193 Nigerian government and Taylor's escape: *New African*, May 2006, 15.

193 Numbers of UN peacekeepers: United Nations Security Council, *Twenty-first Report of the Secretary General on the United Nations Mission in Sierra Leone*, par. 3; United Nations Security Council, *Twenty-fourth Report of the Secretary General on the United Nations Mission in Sierra Leone*, par. 8.

194 "proper governance...": Sierra Leone Truth and Reconciliation Commission, vol. 2, chap. 1, par. 21.

194 "worsening youth...": United Nations Security Council, *First Report of the Secretary General on the United Nations Integrated Office in Sierra Leone*, par. 13.

Sources

Abdullah, Ibrahim. "Bush Path to Destruction: the Origin and Character of the Revolutionary United Front/Sierra Leone." *The Journal of Modern African Studies* 36, no. 2 (1998): 203–35.

Abdullah, Ibrahim and Patrick Muana. "The Revolutionary United Front of Sierra Leone." In *African Guerrillas*, edited by Christopher Clapham, 172–93. Oxford: James Currey, 1998.

Amolo, Milcah. "Trade Unionism and Colonial Authority [in] Sierra Leone: 1930–1945." *Transafrican Journal of History* 8, no. 1 and 2 (1979): 36–52.

Arnold, Guy. *Mercenaries: The Scourge of the Third World*. New York: St. Martin's Press, 1999.

Berkeley, Bill. *The Graves Are Not Yet Full*. New York: Basic Books, 2001.

Cilliers, Jakkie, and Peggy Mason, eds. *Peace, Profit or Plunder?: The Privatisation of Security in War-Torn African Societies*. Pretoria: Institute for Security Studies; Ottawa: Canadian Council for International Peace and Security, 1999.

Coll, Steve. "The Other War." *Washington Post Magazine*, Jan. 9, 2000, 8.

Cox, Thomas S. *Civil-Military Relations in Sierra Leone: A Case Study of African Soldiers in Politics*. Cambridge: Harvard University Press, 1976.

Curtin, Philip D. *The Atlantic Slave Trade: A Census*. Madison: University of Wisconsin Press, 1969.

Divine, Robert C. *Immigration Practice*. 1998 ed. Charlottesville, Va.: Lexis Law Publishing, 1998.

Ellis, Stephen. "Liberia 1989–1994: A Study of Ethnic and Spiritual Violence." *African Affairs* 94 (1995): 165–197.

———. "Liberia's Warlord Insurgency." In *African Guerrillas*, edited by Christopher Clapham, 155–71. Oxford: James Currey, 1998.

Finnegan, R.H. *Survey of the Limba People of Northern Sierra Leone.* London: Her Majesty's Stationery Office, 1965.

Foray, Cyril P. *Historical Dictionary of Sierra Leone.* Metuchen, N.J.: Scarecrow Press, 1977.

Fyfe, Christopher. *A History of Sierra Leone.* London: Oxford University Press, 1962.

Fyle, C. Magbaily. *Almamy Suluku of Sierra Leone c. 1820–1906: The Dynamicis of Political Leadership in Pre-colonial Sierra Leone.* London: Evans Brothers Ltd., 1979.

———, ed. *The State and the Provision of Social Services in Sierra Leone Since Independence, 1961–91.* Dakar, Senegal: CODESRIA, 1993.

———. "The Military and Civil Society in Sierra Leone: The 1992 Military Coup d'Etat." *Africa Development* 19, no. 2 (1994): 127–46.

Gberie, Lansana. *War and Peace in Sierra Leone: Diamonds, Corruption and the Lebanese Connection* (Diamonds and Human Security Project Occasional Paper 6). Ottawa: Partnership Africa Canada, Nov. 2002. *See also,* Levin; Smillie.

Global Witness. *For a Few Dollars More.* London: Global Witness, 2003.

Handbook of Freetown. Freetown: Town Clerk's Office, 1980.

Hayward, Fred M. "Sierra Leone: State Consolidation, Fragmentation and Decay." In *Contemporary West African States*, edited by Donal B. Cruise O'Brien, 165–80. New York: Cambridge University Press, 1989.

Hirsch, John L. *Sierra Leone: Diamonds and the Struggle for Democracy.* Boulder, Colo.: Lynne Rienner, 2001.

Human Rights Watch. *"We'll Kill You if You Cry": Sexual Violence in the Sierra Leone Conflict* 15, no.1 (A). New York: Human Rights Watch, January 2003 (inside pages dated January 2002).

International Crisis Group. *Sierra Leone: Managing Uncertainty* (Africa Report 35). Freetown/Brussels: ICG, Oct. 24, 2001.

———. *Sierra Leone After Elections: Politics as Usual?* (Africa Report 49). Freetown/Brussels: ICG, July 12, 2002.

———. *Sierra Leone's Truth and Reconciliation Commission: A Fresh Start?* (Africa Briefing). Freetown/Brussels: ICG, Dec. 20, 2002.

Koroma, Abdul K. *Sierra Leone: The Agony of a Nation.* Freetown: Andromeda Publications, 1996.

Levin, Estelle A. and Lansana Gberie. *Dealing for Development? The Dynamics of Diamond Marketing and Pricing in Sierra Leone* (Summary Version). Partnership Africa Canada (for the Diamond Development Initiative), March 2006. *See also,* Gberie; Smillie.

Lewis, Roy. *Sierra Leone: A Modern Portrait.* London: Her Majesty's Stationery Office, 1954.

Lizza, Ryan. "Where Angels Fear to Tread." *New Republic,* July 24, 2000, 22–27.

MacKenzie, S.W. "Rent-A-Gurkha: Crown's Finest Fighters for Hire." *Soldier of Fortune,* March 1994, 30.

MacKenzie, Sibyl. "Death of a Warrior." *Soldier of Fortune,* July 1995, 36.

Malan, Mark, Phenyo Rakate, and Angela McIntyre. *Peacekeeping in Sierra Leone: UNAMSIL Hits the Home Straight* (Monograph 68). Pretoria: Institute for Security Studies, Jan. 2002.

Muana, Patrick K. "The Kamajoi Militia: Civil War, Internal Displacement and the Politics of Counter-Insurgency." *Africa Development* 22, nos. 3/4 (1997): 77–100.

Pakenham, Thomas. *The Scramble for Africa.* New York: Random House, 1991.

Peters, Krijn and Paul Richards. "'Why We Fight': Voices of Youth Combatants in Sierra Leone." *Africa* 68, no. 2 (1998): 183–210.

Physicians for Human Rights. *War-Related Sexual Violence in Sierra Leone: A Population-Based Assessment.* Boston: PHR, 2002.

Porter, Arthur T. *Creoledom: A Study of the Development of Freetown Society.* London: Oxford University Press, 1963.

Rashid, Ishmail. "Subaltern Reactions: Lumpens, Students, and the Left." *Africa Development* 22, nos. 3/4 (1997): 19–43.

Reno, William. *Corruption and State Politics in Sierra Leone.* Cambridge: Cambridge University Press, 1995.

——. *Warlord Politics and African States.* Boulder, Colo.: Lynne Rienner, 1998.

Revolutionary United Front, "Footpaths to Democracy: Toward a New Sierra Leone." N.p. [1995].

Richards, Paul. "Anarchists or Catalysts?" *West Africa*, Feb. 20, 1995, 265–66.

——. *Fighting for the Rain Forest: War, Youth & Resources in Sierra Leone.* Oxford: James Currey, 1996.

Roberts, George O. *The Anguish of Third World Independence: The Sierra Leone Experience.* Lanham, Md.: University Press of America, 1982.

Rubin, Elizabeth. "An Army of One's Own." *Harper's Magazine*, Feb. 1997, 44–55.

Sierra Leone Truth and Reconciliation Commission. *Witness to Truth: Report of the Sierra Leone Truth and Reconciliation Commission.* Freetown: Sierra Leone Truth and Reconciliation Commission, 2004 (report can be found at http://trcsierraleone.org).

Sierra Leone Yearbook 1965. Freetown: Daily Mail, 1965.

Smillie, Ian, Lansana Gberie, and Ralph Hazleton. *The Heart of the Matter: Sierra Leone, Diamonds & Human Security.* Ottawa: Partnership Africa Canada, 2000.

Smillie, Ian. *The Kimberley Process: The Case for Monitoring* (Diamonds and Human Security Project Occasional Paper #5). Ottawa: Partnership Africa Canada, 2002.

Spitzer, Leo and LaRay Denzer. "I. T.A. Wallace-Johnson and the West African Youth League." *The International Journal of African Historical Studies* 6, no. 3 (1973): 413–52.

Stevens, Siaka Probyn. *What Life Has Taught Me.* Bourne End, England: Kensal Press, 1984.

UNICEF. *The State of the World's Children 2004.* New York: UNICEF, 2004.

United Nations Security Council. *First Report of the Secretary-General on the United Nations Integrated Office in Sierra Leone* (S/2006/269). New York: UN Security Council, April 28, 2006.

——. … *Progress Report of the Secretary-General on the United Nations Mission in Liberia, Ninth* (S/2005/764); *Tenth* (S/2006/159); *Eleventh* (S/2006/376). New York: UN Security Council, 2005–2006.

——. *Report of the Panel of Experts Pursuant to Security Council Resolution 1306 (2000), Paragraph 19, in Relation to Sierra Leone* (S/2000/1195). New York: UN Security Council, Dec. 20, 2000.

——. … *Report of the Secretary-General on the United Nations Mission in Sierra Leone, Twelfth* (S/2001/1195); *Thirteenth* (S/2002/267); *Fourteenth* (S/2002/679); *Fifteenth* (S/2002/987); *Sixteenth* (S/2002/1417); *Seventeenth* (S/2003/321); *Eighteenth* (S/2003/663); *Nineteenth* (S/2003/863); *Twentieth* (S/2003/1201); *Twenty-first* (S/2004/228); *Twenty-second* (S/2004/536); *Twenty-third* (S/2004/724); *Twenty-fourth* (S/2004/965); *Twenty-fifth* (S/2005/273); *Twenty-sixth* (S/2005/596); *Twenty-seventh* (S/2005/777). New York: UN Security Council, 2001–2005.

——. *Seventh Report of the Secretary-General on the United Nations Observer Mission in Sierra Leone* (S/1999/836). New York: UN Security Council, July 30, 1999.

U.S. Committee for Refugees. *USCR Site Visit to Sierra Leone & Guinea (August–September 1999).* Washington, DC: USCR, Sept. 16, 1999.

Van Der Laan, H.L. *The Sierra Leone Diamonds: An Economic Study Covering the Years 1952–1961.* London: Oxford University Press, 1965.

Zack-Williams, A.B. "Kamajors, 'Sobel' & the Militariat: Civil Society & the Return of the Military in Sierra Leone Politics." *Review of African Political Economy* 73 (1997): 373–80.

Index